10

MINUTE GUIDE TO

EXCEL FOR WINDOWS® 95

by Trudi Reisner

A Division of Macmillan Computer Publishing USA
201 West 103rd St., Indianapolis, Indiana 46290

To Anne Gallo. Thank you for all the support and understanding.

©1995 by Que® Corporation

International Standard Book Number: 0-7897-0373-4

Library of Congress Catalog Card Number: 94-73407

98   8 7 6

Interpretation of the printing code: the rightmost number of the first series of numbers is the year of the book's printing; the rightmost number of the second series of numbers is the number of the book's printing. For example, a printing code of 95-1 shows that the first printing of the book occurred in 1995.

Printed in the United States of America

Publisher Roland Elgey

Vice President and Publisher Marie Butler-Knight

Editorial Services Director Elizabeth Keaffaber

Publishing Manager Barry Pruett

Managing Editor Michael Cunningham

Development Editor Lori Cates

Production Editor Mark Enochs

Copy Editor Paige Widder

Cover Designer Dan Armstrong

Book Designer Kim Scott

Technical Specialist Cari Skaggs

Indexer Christopher Cleveland

Production Angela D. Bannan, Michael Brumitt, Charlotte Clapp, Jeanne Clark, Mike Dietsch, Terri Edwards, Louisa Klucznik, Nancy Price, Brian-Kent Proffitt, Bobbi Satterfield, SA Springer

Special thanks to Martin Wyatt for ensuring the technical accuracy of this book.

CONTENTS

INTRODUCTION

Perhaps you walked into work this morning and found Excel for Windows 95 on your desk. A note is stuck to the box: "We need a budget report for the upcoming meeting. See what you can do."

NOW WHAT?

You could wade through the manuals that came with the program to find out how to perform a specific task, but that may take a while, and it may tell you more than you want to know. You need a practical guide, one that will tell you exactly how to create and print the worksheets, reports, and graphs you need for the meeting.

WELCOME TO THE *10 MINUTE GUIDE TO EXCEL FOR WINDOWS 95*

Because most people don't have the luxury of sitting down uninterrupted for hours at a time to learn Excel, this *10 Minute Guide* does not attempt to teach everything about the program. Instead, it focuses on the most often-used features. Each feature is covered in self-contained lessons, which are designed to take 10 minutes or less to complete.

The *10 Minute Guide* teaches you about the program without relying on technical jargon. With straightforward, easy-to-follow explanations and lists of numbered steps that tell you what keys to press and what options to select, the *10 Minute Guide to Excel for Windows 95* makes learning the program quick and easy.

WHO SHOULD USE THE *10 MINUTE GUIDE TO EXCEL FOR WINDOWS 95?*

The *10 Minute Guide to Excel for Windows 95* is for anyone who

- Needs to learn Excel quickly.

- Feels overwhelmed or intimidated by the complexity of Excel.

- Wants to find out quickly whether Excel for Windows 95 will meet his or her computing needs.

- Wants a clear, concise guide to the most important features of Excel for Windows 95.

HOW TO USE THIS BOOK

The *10 Minute Guide to Excel for Windows 95* consists of a series of lessons ranging from basic startup to a few more advanced features. If this is your first encounter with Excel for Windows 95, you should probably work through Lessons 1 to 15 in order. These lessons lead you through the process of creating, editing, and printing a spreadsheet. Subsequent lessons tell you how to use the more advanced features to customize your spreadsheet; use your spreadsheet as a database; create and print graphs (charts); and generate reports.

If Excel for Windows 95 has not been installed on your computer, consult the inside front cover for installation steps.

ICONS AND CONVENTIONS USED IN THIS BOOK

The following icons have been added throughout the book to help you find your way around:

Timesaver Tip icons offer shortcuts and hints for using the program efficiently.

 Plain English icons define new terms.

 Panic Button icons appear where new users often run into trouble.

 In addition, Excel version 95 icons help you identify features that are new to Microsoft Excel for Windows 95. You can quickly take advantage of the latest timesaving features of the latest version of Excel.

The following conventions have been used to clarify the steps you must perform:

On-screen text   Any text that appears on-screen is shown in bold.

What you type The information you type appears in bold and in color.

Menu names   The names of menus, commands, buttons, and dialog boxes are shown with the first letter capitalized for easy recognition.

Key+Key Combinations   In many cases, you must press a two-key combination to enter a command. For example, "Press Alt+X." In such cases, hold down the first key while pressing the second key.

By Any Other Name   Excel for Windows 95 was designed to work with the Windows 95 operating system. It is also sometimes known as Excel 7, although the last version of Excel was known as Excel 5 (Microsoft skipped a number so that all its Office applications would have the same version number). In this book, we refer to the newest version as "Excel for Windows 95," "Excel 95," and just "Excel."

ACKNOWLEDGMENTS

Many thanks to the people at Que who have helped me with this project. First, thanks to Martha O'Sullivan, Acquisitions Editor, for signing me to write this. Thanks to Lori Cates, Product Development Specialist, for her help with developing this book. Thanks to Mark Enochs, Production Editor, for keeping the manuscript in great shape. And thanks to all the other people I worked with at Que who helped turn this book around on such an aggressive schedule.

TRADEMARKS

All terms mentioned in this book that are known to be trademarks or service marks are listed below. In addition, terms suspected of being trademarks or service marks have been appropriately capitalized. Que cannot attest to the accuracy of this information. Use of a term in this book should not be regarded as affecting the validity of any trademark or service mark.

MS-DOS, Windows, Excel, and Toolbar are trademarks of Microsoft Corporation.

STARTING AND EXITING EXCEL

In this lesson, you'll learn how to start and end a typical Excel work session and how to get online help.

STARTING EXCEL

To use Excel, you must master some basic techniques in Microsoft Windows 95, including opening windows, running applications, dragging, and scrolling. If these terms are unfamiliar to you, refer to the Windows 95 Primer at the back of this book before moving on.

After you installed Excel (see the inside front cover of this book), the installation program returned you to the desktop. To start Excel, follow these steps:

1. Click the Start button. The Start menu appears.

2. Choose Programs. The Programs menu appears, as shown in Figure 1.1.

3. Choose the Microsoft Excel program item to start the program.

The Excel opening screen appears (see Figure 1.2) with a blank workbook labeled Book1. Excel is now ready for you to begin creating your workbook.

You will perform most operations in Excel by using the menu bar, at the top of the screen, and the Standard toolbar, just below it. In the next two lessons, you'll learn about the various operations available from the menu bar and the Standard toolbar.

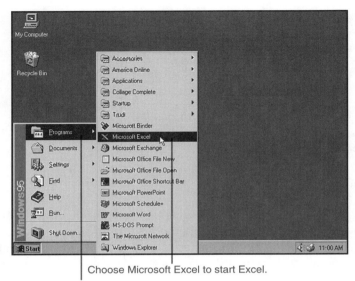

Choose Microsoft Excel to start Excel.

Choose Programs on the Start menu.

FIGURE 1.1   Select the Microsoft Excel program item to start the program.

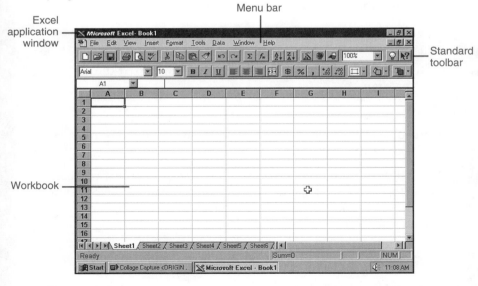

FIGURE 1.2   Excel's opening screen displays a blank workbook named Book1.

Workbook   An Excel file is called a *workbook*. Each workbook consists of 16 worksheets. Each worksheet consists of columns and rows that intersect to form boxes called *cells* into which you enter text. The tabs at the bottom of the workbook (which are labeled Sheet1, Sheet2, and so on) let you flip through the worksheets when you click on them with the mouse.

Newly Styled Components   For the most part, the components in the Excel for Windows 95 and Excel 5 window are the same. The main difference is that the title bar, the Minimize, Maximize, and Restore buttons, and the Control menu have a new look in Excel for Windows 95. Also, the windows have a Close button (in the top right corner, marked with an x) that lets you close the window with just one click.

GETTING HELP

You can get help in Excel in three different ways:

Pull down the Help menu. Pull down the Help menu for various help options. You can then select Microsoft Excel Help Topics (for groups of help topics), Answer Wizard (to search for a specific topic), The Microsoft Network (for specific details on how to work with Excel and the Microsoft Network), Lotus 1-2-3 Help (for specific details on how to make the transition from this program), or About Microsoft Excel (for licensing and system information and technical support for Excel from Microsoft).

Click on the Help button. The Help button is in the Standard toolbar; it's the button that has the arrow and the question mark on it. When you click on the Help button, the mouse pointer turns into an arrow with a question mark. Click on any item or part of the screen with which you need help, and Excel displays help for that item or screen area. Double-click on the Help button to search for a Help topic.

Click on the What's This? button in a dialog box. The What's This? button appears in the upper right corner of a dialog box. It's the button that has a question mark on it. When you click on this button, the mouse pointer turns into an arrow with a question mark. Click on any item in the dialog box with which you need help, and Excel displays a pop-up box that contains information about that item. To close the Help box, click anywhere on the screen or press the Esc key.

> **TIP** **Quick Description** You also can right-click an option in a dialog box to see a description of the selected option.

GETTING AROUND IN A HELP WINDOW

When you choose Help, Microsoft Excel Help Topics in the menu bar, Excel displays a Help window like the one in Figure 1.3. The Help window is organized like a reference book with four tabs: Contents, Index, Find, and Answer Wizard.

- **Contents** displays groups of Help topics. The Contents feature is a table of contents that shows top level chapters with a short description of the book's chapter. As you can see in Figure 1.3, a chapter is represented by a book icon, and a subtopic is represented by a page (with a question mark) icon. Select a book to see a list of the subtopics. Select a subtopic and then click the Open button to see the Help information in a Help window. Many chapters have Tips and Tricks and Troubleshooting subtopics, which are each represented with a page icon at the bottom of a list of subtopics.

- **Index** displays a comprehensive list of Help topics in alphabetical order. To quickly find information on a particular topic, you can use Help's Index feature. For example, type **copying** in the Topic text box and press

Enter. Excel displays one or more topics (related to the desired topic) in the Topic list. If you want information about a topic, click the topic. Then click the Display button, and Excel displays the selected Help topic information in a Help window. Index is especially useful when you cannot find a particular Help topic in Help Contents' list of topics.

- **Find** allows you to search for a particular word in a Help topic rather than search for a Help topic by category. First, you have to instruct Excel to create a list which contains every word from your Help files. You only have to create the word list once. Then you can search for words and phrases similar to existing words and phrases in a Help topic. You type a word, and Excel suggests similar words that are within Help. Then you click on one of these suggested words, and Excel suggests topics related to the selected word. Double-click on a topic to display the help information.

Accidents Happen If you don't want to use the first list that Excel created, don't worry. You can rebuild that list to include more words or exclude words from the list. Click the Rebuild button and choose a word list option to re-create the word list.

- **Answer Wizard** enables you to find the solution to a help request. First, you type a request in your own words in the text box at the top of the Answer Wizard. For example, type **copy formulas.** Then click the Search button. Excel displays the topics in the topics list that relate to the request you made. Select a topic from the list and then click the Display button. The Answer Wizard gives you step-by-step explanations while you work. Rather than search for a Help topic by category or specific words and phrases, you can use the Answer Wizard to learn the exact steps you need to follow to get a task done.

Index tab

Contents tab | Find tab

Chapter
book
icon

Subtopic
page
icon

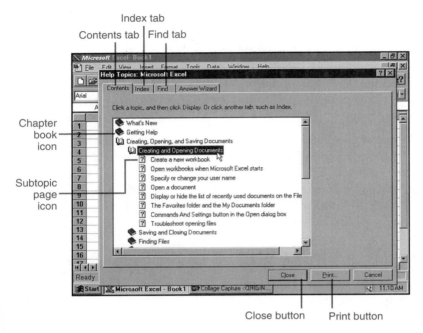

Close button   Print button

FIGURE 1.3   The Help Topics: Microsoft Excel window.

If you want to print the list of help topics in the Help Topics: Microsoft Excel window, click the Print button at the bottom of the window. The Print dialog box appears. Click the OK button to print the list of help topics and subtopics in the Help Topics: Microsoft Excel window.

When you open a page in a chapter, a Help menu bar appears at the top of the Help window (see Figure 1.4). The Help menu bar includes three buttons: Help Topics, Back, and Options.

Help Topics   Returns you to Help's table of contents.

Back   Closes the current Help window and returns to the preceding one.

Options   Displays a menu with the following commands: Annotate, Copy, Print Topic, Font, Keep Help on Top, Use System Colors, and Help Version.

Wrong Place at the Wrong Time   If you accidentally select the wrong Help topic, don't worry. You can always click the Help Topics button on the Help toolbar, and then select the correct Help topic.

Most Help windows contain terms or topics that are underlined with a dotted line. These are called *jumps*. If you click on a dotted underlined word, Excel displays a pop-up text box that provides a bit more information about the term.

Some Help windows contain shortcut buttons that allow you to jump to the area of Excel to which the Help information refers. A shortcut button contains two right arrowheads. For example, suppose you're reading a Help topic that contains information on how to select cells in a worksheet. You click the Shortcut button to jump to the Help window that contains more information on selecting cells in a worksheet.

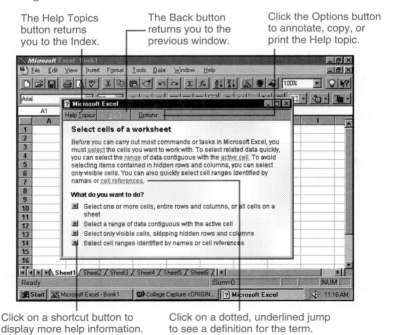

The Help Topics button returns you to the Index.

The Back button returns you to the previous window.

Click the Options button to annotate, copy, or print the Help topic.

Click on a shortcut button to display more help information.

Click on a dotted, underlined jump to see a definition for the term.

FIGURE 1.4   An Excel Help window.

Fast Help   You also can press F1 to get help on a menu command or an item in a dialog box. Place your mouse pointer over the item you want help on, then press F1.

New and Improved Help   Excel for Windows 95 and Excel 5 Help are organized differently. Excel for Windows 95 has the main functions Contents, Index, Find, and the Answer Wizard. Excel 5 contains the main functions Contents, Search, and Glossary. Also, you no longer have to scroll the Help window by clicking the scroll arrows because the list of Help topics is short; the topics all fit on one small screen.

To exit Help, perform any of the following steps:

- Press Alt+F4, or double-click on the Close button in the upper right corner of the Help window.

- Press Alt+F, or click on File in the Help window, and select Exit (or press X).

- Click the Close button in the upper right corner of the Help window.

To move the Help window out of the way without closing it, click on the Minimize button in the upper right corner of the Help window. This shrinks the window down to a button on the Taskbar. To get the help window back, click on the ? Microsoft Excel button on the Taskbar.

DISCOVERING MORE WITH THE TIPWIZARD

Excel's TipWizard shows you a few of the many shortcuts in Excel. The TipWizard gives you pointers or shortcuts on how to perform a command. For example, if you are summing a group of numbers, an alternate way to sum numbers displays in the TipWizard box.

To use the TipWizard, follow these steps:

1. Click the TipWizard button on the Standard toolbar, as shown in Figure 1.5. This button turns the TipWizard on or off.

2. After you perform any commands, you can click the down arrow button at the end of the TipWizard box, located beneath the Formatting toolbar. The down arrow button displays the next tip.

3. Click the up arrow button at the end of the TipWizard box. The up arrow button displays the previous tip.

4. If a tip suggests clicking a button on a toolbar, the button displays at the end of the TipWizard box. You can click the button at the end of the TipWizard box to try the TipWizard's suggestion.

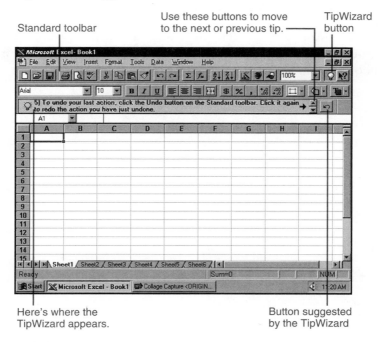

FIGURE 1.5 The TipWizard offers timesaving advice.

EXITING EXCEL

To exit Excel and return to the Windows 95 desktop, follow these steps:

1. Press Alt+F or click on File on the menu bar.

2. Press X, or click on Exit.

If you changed the workbook in any way without saving the file, Excel will display a prompt asking if you want to save the file before exiting. Select the desired option.

 Quick Exit For a quick exit, press Alt+F4, or double-click on the Control-menu in the upper left corner of the Excel window. You can also click the Close (X) button in the upper right corner of the Excel window.

In this lesson, you learned how to enter and exit Excel and get online help. In the next lesson, you'll learn about the Excel workbook window.

EXAMINING THE EXCEL WINDOW

In this lesson, you'll learn the basics of moving around in the Excel window and in the workbook window.

NAVIGATING THE EXCEL WINDOW

As you can see in Figure 2.1, the Excel window contains several elements that allow you to enter commands and data:

Menu bar Displays the names of the available pull-down menus. When you select a menu, it drops down over a portion of the screen, presenting you with a list of options.

Toolbars Contain several icons, buttons, and drop-down lists that give you quick access to often-used commands and features. The Standard and Formatting toolbars appear at the top of the Excel window. If you are using Excel as part of Microsoft Office 95, you will see the Microsoft Office toolbar in the upper right corner of the screen. If you are using Windows for Workgroups, you will see the Workgroup toolbar near the top of the left side of your screen. The screen pictures in this book do not include either of these particular toolbars.

Formula bar To enter information in a cell, you select the cell and type the information in the cell. The data appears in the cell and in the formula bar as you type. When you press Enter, the information is inserted in the selected cell.

Workbook window Contains the workbook where you will enter the data and formulas that make up your workbook and the worksheets it contains.

Status bar Displays information about the current activity, including help information and keyboard and program modes. A keyboard mode, for example, is the CAPS indicator on the status bar which tells you that your CAPS LOCK key is on. A program mode such as READY indicates that Excel is ready for you to enter data or perform a command.

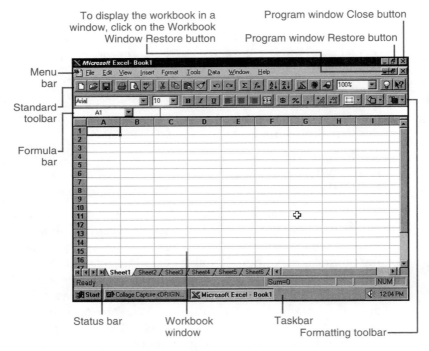

FIGURE 2.1 Elements of the Excel window.

NAVIGATING THE WORKBOOK WINDOW

Inside the Excel program window is a workbook window with the current worksheet in front. In this window, you will enter the labels (text), values (numbers), and formulas (calculations) that make up each worksheet. Figure 2.2 illustrates the various parts of the workbook. Table 2.1 describes these parts.

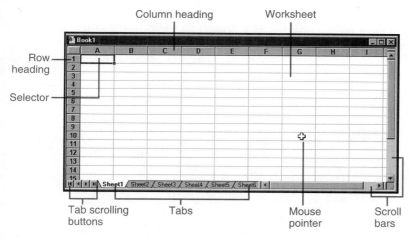

FIGURE 2.2   Elements of the workbook window.

TABLE 2.1   WORKBOOK WINDOW ITEMS

ITEM	FUNCTION
Tabs	A workbook starts with 16 worksheets, and you can add or delete sheets as needed. You can use the tabs to flip worksheets.
Tab scrolling buttons	Allow you to scroll through the worksheets in the workbook.
Scroll bars	Allow you to view a section of the current worksheet that is not displayed.
Column heading	Identifies the column by letters.
Row heading	Identifies the row by numbers.

continues

TABLE 2.1   CONTINUED

ITEM	FUNCTION
Selector	Outline that indicates the active cell (the one in which you are working).
Split bars	Let you split the workbook window into more than one pane to view different portions of the same worksheet.

What's a Cell?   Each page in a workbook is a separate worksheet. Each worksheet contains a grid consisting of alphabetized columns and numbered rows. When a row and column intersect, they form a box called a *cell*. Each cell has an *address* that consists of the column letter and row number (A1, B3, C4, and so on).

FLIPPING WORKSHEETS

Because each workbook consists of 16 worksheets, you need a way to move from worksheet to worksheet. If you are using the keyboard, you can flip among worksheets by pressing Ctrl+PgDn and Ctrl+PgUp.

If you are using the mouse, there are easier ways to flip worksheets. If a tab is shown for the worksheet you want to move to, click on the tab for that worksheet (see Figure 2.3). If the tab is not shown, use the scroll buttons to bring the tab into view, and then click on the tab.

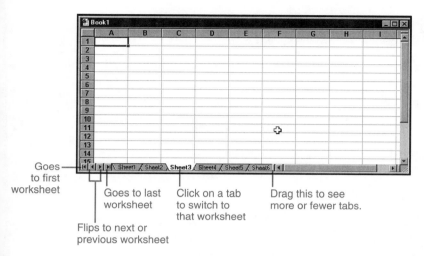

Goes to first worksheet

Goes to last worksheet

Flips to next or previous worksheet

Click on a tab to switch to that worksheet

Drag this to see more or fewer tabs.

FIGURE 2.3   You can move from worksheet to worksheet with tabs.

MOVING ON A WORKSHEET

Once the worksheet you want to work on is displayed, you need some way of moving to the various cells on the worksheet. Keep in mind that the part of the worksheet displayed on-screen is only a small part of the worksheet, as illustrated in Figure 2.4.

To move around the worksheet with your keyboard, use the keys as described in Table 2.2.

TABLE 2.2   MOVING AROUND A WORKSHEET WITH THE KEYBOARD

PRESS	TO MOVE
↑ ↓ ← →	One cell in the direction of the arrow.
Ctrl+↑ or Ctrl+↓	To the top or bottom of a data region (an area of the worksheet that contains data).

continues

TABLE 2.2   CONTINUED

PRESS	TO MOVE
Ctrl+← or Ctrl+→	To the leftmost or rightmost cell in a data region.
PgUp	Up one screen.
PgDn	Down one screen.
Home	Leftmost cell in a row.
Ctrl+Home	Upper left corner of a worksheet.
Ctrl+End	Lower left corner of a worksheet.
End+↑, End+↓, End+←, End+→	If the active cell is blank, moves to the next blank cell in the direction of the arrow. If the active cell contains an entry, moves in the direction of the arrow to the next cell that has an entry.
End+Enter	Last column in row.

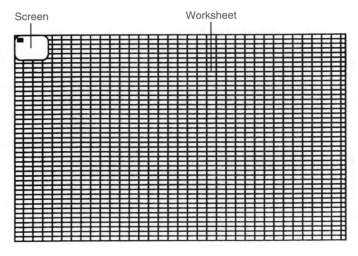

FIGURE 2.4   The worksheet area displayed on-screen is a small portion of the worksheet.

If you have a mouse, moving on a worksheet is easier. Use the scroll bars to scroll to the area of the screen that contains the cell you want to work with. Then, click on the cell. To use the scroll bars:

- Click once on a scroll arrow at the end of the scroll bar to scroll incrementally in the direction of the arrow. Hold down the mouse button to scroll continuously.

- Drag the scroll box inside the scroll bar to the area of the worksheet you want to view. For example, to move to the middle of the worksheet, drag the scroll box to the middle of the scroll bar.

- Click once inside the scroll bar, on either side of the scroll box, to move the view one screenful at a time.

TIP **F5 (Goto) for Quick Movement!**   To move to a specific cell on a worksheet, pull down the Edit menu and select Go To, or press F5. Type the cell's address in the Reference text box; the address consists of the column letter and row number that define the location of the cell, for example **m25**. To go to a cell on a specific page, type the page name, an exclamation point, and the cell address (for example, **sheet3!m25**). Click on the OK button.

In this lesson, you learned how to move around in the Excel window and move around in workbooks. In the next lesson, you will learn how to use Excel's toolbars.

3 USING EXCEL'S TOOLBARS

In this lesson, you will learn how to use Excel's toolbars to save time when you work. You will also learn how to arrange them for maximum performance.

USING THE TOOLBARS

Unless you tell it otherwise, Excel displays the Standard and Formatting toolbars as shown in Figure 3.1. To select a tool from a toolbar, click on that tool.

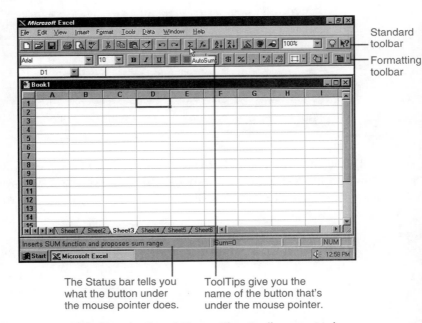

The Status bar tells you what the button under the mouse pointer does.

ToolTips give you the name of the button that's under the mouse pointer.

FIGURE 3.1 The Standard and Formatting toolbars contain buttons for Excel's most commonly used features.

What Is a Toolbar?   An Excel toolbar is a collection of tools or shortcut icons displayed in a long bar that can be moved and reshaped to make it more convenient for you to use.

LEARNING MORE ABOUT TOOLBAR BUTTONS

The following tables show you all the tools in the Standard and Formatting toolbars.

TABLE 3.1   EXCEL STANDARD TOOLBAR BUTTONS

BUTTON	NAME	DESCRIPTION
	New Workbook	Creates a new workbook.
	Open	Opens an existing work-book.
	Save	Saves the workbook.
	Print	Prints the workbook.
	Print Preview	Changes to print preview.
	Spelling	Starts the Spelling checker.
	Cut	Cuts selected ranges to the Clipboard.
	Copy	Copies selected range to the Clipboard.

continues

TABLE 3.1   CONTINUED

BUTTON	NAME	DESCRIPTION
	Paste	Pastes data from the Clipboard.
	Format Painter	Copies formatting.
	Undo	Undoes last command.
	Repeat	Repeats last command.
	AutoSum	Creates a sum function.
	Function Wizard	Starts the FunctionWizard.
	Sort Ascending	Sorts selection in ascending order.
	Sort Descending	Sorts selection in descending order.
	ChartWizard	Starts the ChartWizard.
	Map	Starts Data Map.
	Drawing	Displays the Drawing toolbar.
	Zoom Control	Enables you to zoom the worksheet to the percent you specify.
	TipWizard	Starts the TipWizard.
	Help	Enables you to get context-sensitive help.

TABLE 3.2 EXCEL FORMATTING TOOLBAR BUTTONS

Button	Name	Description
	Font	Enables you to select a font from drop-down list.
	Font Size	Enables you to select a font size from drop-down list.
B	Bold	Applies bold to selected range.
I	Italic	Applies italic to selected range.
U	Underline	Underlines selected range.
	Align Left	Aligns selected range to the left.
	Center	Centers selected range.
	Align Right	Aligns selected range to the right.
	Center Across Columns	Centers text across selected range.
$	Currency Style	Applies currency style to the selected range.
%	Percent Style	Applies percent style to the selected range.
,	Comma Style	Applies comma style to the selected range.
	Increase Decimal	Increases the number of decimal points displayed in the selected range.

continues

TABLE 3.2   CONTINUED

BUTTON	NAME	DESCRIPTION
	Decrease Decimal	Decreases the number of decimal points displayed in the selected range.
	Borders	Enables you to select and apply borders to selected range.
	Color	Enables you to select and apply color to selected range.
	Font Color	Enables you to select and apply color to text in selected range.

In addition to the tools on the Standard and Formatting toolbars, there are other toolbars that contain tools in Excel. Here are some easy ways to learn about the buttons for yourself:

- To see the name of a button, move the mouse pointer over the button. Excel displays a *ToolTip* that provides the name of the button, as shown in Figure 3.1.

- To learn what a button does, move the mouse pointer over the button and look at the status bar (at the bottom of the screen—see fig. 3.1). If the button is available for the task you are currently performing, Excel displays a description of what the button does.

- To learn more about a button, click on the Help button in the Standard toolbar (the button with the arrow and question mark), and then click on the button for which you want more information.

TURNING TOOLBARS ON OR OFF

Excel initially displays the Standard and Formatting toolbars. If you never use one of these toolbars, you can turn one or both of them off. In addition, you can turn a toolbar on or off by using the View Toolbars command or the shortcut menu.

To use the View Toolbars option:

1. Open the View menu, and choose Toolbars. The Toolbars dialog box appears, as shown in Figure 3.2.

2. Select the toolbar(s) you would like to hide or display. A check mark in the toolbar's check box means the toolbar will be displayed. A blank box means the toolbar will be hidden.

3. Click OK to accept the toolbar changes.

Workgroup Toolbar   When you first open Excel, you may see an extra toolbar, called the WorkGroup toolbar. This toolbar includes buttons that allow you to perform tasks in a networked environment, which are not discussed in this book. To remove this toolbar, click on View in the main menu bar. Then click on Toolbars. In the Toolbars dialog box, click on the WorkGroup check box to remove the check. Click OK and the toolbar disappears.

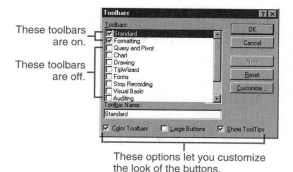

These toolbars are on.

These toolbars are off.

These options let you customize the look of the buttons.

FIGURE 3.2   Use the Toolbars dialog box to display toolbars.

To use the shortcut menu to hide or display a toolbar, follow these steps:

1. Move the mouse pointer anywhere inside any toolbar.

2. Click the right mouse button. The Toolbars shortcut menu appears.

3. Click on a toolbar name to turn it off. To display a toolbar, click on a toolbar name that doesn't have a check mark next to it. Excel places a check mark next to the name of a displayed toolbar.

MOVING TOOLBARS

After you have displayed the toolbars you need, you may position them in your work area where they are most convenient. Figure 3.3 shows an Excel screen with three toolbars in various positions.

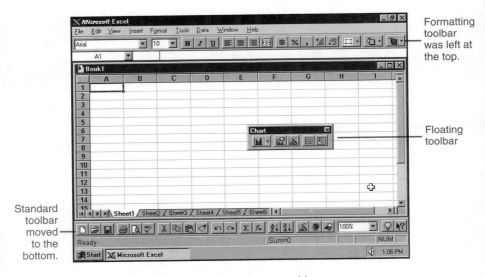

Formatting toolbar was left at the top.

Floating toolbar

Standard toolbar moved to the bottom.

FIGURE 3.3 Three toolbars in various positions.

Here's what you do to move a toolbar:

1. Move the mouse pointer over a buttonless part of the toolbar.

2. Hold down the mouse button and drag the toolbar where you want it. You can drag it to a dock or let it "float" anywhere in the window.

If you decide to drag the toolbar to a dock, you can position it in one of four toolbar docks: between the formula bar and menu bar, on the left and right sides of the Excel window, and at the bottom of the Excel window. You'll know that you've found a dock when the toolbar outline changes from square to rectangular. Then you can release the mouse button. If a toolbar contains a drop-down list (such as the Zoom Control tool in the Standard toolbar and the Font tool in the Formatting toolbar), you cannot drag it to a left or right toolbar dock.

CUSTOMIZING THE TOOLBARS

If Excel's toolbars provide too few (or too many) options for you, you can create your own toolbars or customize existing toolbars. To make your own toolbar, do this:

1. Open the View menu, and choose Toolbars.

2. In the Toolbar Name text box, type the name you want to give your toolbar. This makes the New button available.

3. Click on the New button. Excel creates a new floating toolbar and displays the Customize dialog box, so you can start adding buttons to your toolbar.

4. Drag the desired buttons onto the toolbar, as shown in Figure 3.4.

5. Select Close.

If you want to delete a custom toolbar, open the View menu, and choose Toolbars. In the Toolbars list, click on the custom toolbar you want to delete, then click on the Delete button in the Toolbars dialog box.

New toolbar will
expand as you drag
buttons onto it.

You can drag buttons off any toolbar to
delete them, or drag them to a different
toolbar to move them.

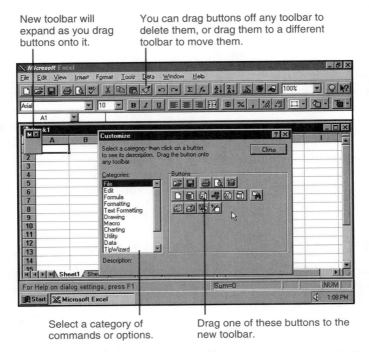

Select a category of
commands or options.

Drag one of these buttons to the
new toolbar.

FIGURE 3.4 Drag buttons from the Customize dialog box to the
new toolbar.

You can add, remove, or change the order of the buttons on any
toolbar (Excel's or your own).

To remove buttons from the toolbar, perform these steps:

1. Do one of the following:

   - Right-click on the toolbar you want to customize,
     and choose Customize.

   - Open the View menu, and choose Toolbars. High-
     light the name of the toolbar you want to custom-
     ize, and choose Customize.

2. Drag the unwanted button off the toolbar.

3. Click on the Close button when you're done.

To add buttons to the toolbar, perform these steps:

1. Do one of the following:

   • Right-click on the toolbar you want to customize, and choose Customize.

   • Open the View menu, and choose Toolbars. Highlight the name of the toolbar you want to customize, and choose Customize.

2. Select the type of tool you want to add from the Categories list. For example, you can add buttons for file commands, formulas, formatting, or macros. You'll see a collection of buttons. Click on a button to view its description at the bottom of the Customize dialog box.

3. Drag the desired button(s) onto a toolbar (any toolbar that's displayed).

4. Click on the Close button when you're done.

To rearrange the buttons on the toolbar, just drag them around within the bar while you are in the Customize dialog box.

 Resetting Toolbars   If you mess up one of Excel's toolbars, you can return to (the way it was before) at a click of the button. Choose View Toolbars, highlight the name of the toolbar you want to reset, and then click on the Reset button.

In this lesson, you learned how to use Excel's toolbars and customize toolbars for your own unique needs. In the next lesson, you will learn how to enter different types of data.

ENTERING DIFFERENT TYPES OF DATA

In this lesson, you will learn how to enter different types of data in an Excel worksheet.

TYPES OF DATA

To create a worksheet that does something, you must enter data into the cells that make up the worksheet. There are many types of data that you can enter, including

- Text
- Numbers
- Dates
- Times
- Formulas
- Functions

ENTERING TEXT

You can enter any combination of letters and numbers as text. Text is automatically left-aligned in a cell.

To enter text into a cell

1. Select the cell into which you want to enter text by clicking the cell.

2. Type the text. As you type, your text appears in the cell and in the formula bar, as shown in Figure 4.1.

3. Click on the Enter button on the formula bar (the button with the check mark on it), or press the Enter key, Tab key, or an arrow key on your keyboard.

ENTERING COLUMN AND ROW HEADINGS

Column headings and row headings are sometimes referred to as titles. The column headings appear across the top of the worksheet beneath the title. The row headings are on the left side of the worksheet, usually in Column A.

Column headings describe what the numbers represent in a column. You can enter column headings to specify time periods such as years, months, days, dates, and so on. Row headings describe what the numbers represent in a row. You can enter row headings to identify income and expense items in a budget, subject titles, and other categories.

To enter column headings into a worksheet

1. Select the cell into which you want to enter the first column heading by clicking the cell.

2. Type the first column heading.

3. Press the Tab key or right arrow key → on your keyboard to move across to the next cell in the row.

4. Repeat steps 2 and 3 until you've entered all your column headings, as shown in Figure 4.1.

To enter row headings into a worksheet

1. Select the cell into which you want to enter the first row heading by clicking the cell.

2. Type the first row heading.

3. Press the Enter key or down arrow key ↓ on your keyboard to move down to the next cell in the column.

4. Repeat steps 2 and 3 until you've entered all your row headings. (See Figure 4.1.)

Sometimes your column and row headings may spill over into the adjacent cells. You can choose the Format Column AutoFit Selection command to widen the column and accommodate the long entries.

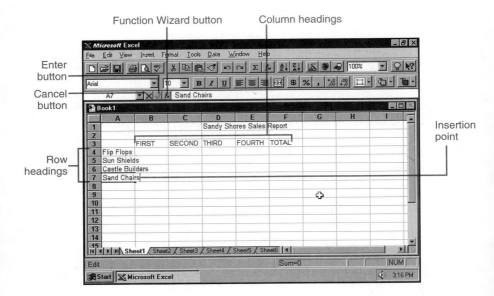

FIGURE 4.1 Data that you enter also appears on the formula bar as you type it.

 TIP **Numbers as Text** You may want to enter a number as text (for example, a ZIP code). Precede your entry with a single quotation mark ('), as in '46220. The single quotation mark is an alignment prefix that tells Excel to treat the following characters as text and left-align them in the cell.

ENTERING NUMBERS

Valid numbers can include the numeric characters 0–9 and any of these special characters: + ( ) , $.%. Numbers are automatically right-aligned. You can include commas, decimal points, dollar signs, percentage signs, and parentheses in the values you enter.

Although you can include punctuation, you may not want to. For example, rather than type a column of dollar amounts including the dollar signs, commas, and decimal points, you can type numbers such as 700 and 81295, and then format the column with currency formatting. Excel would then change your entries to $700.00 and 81,295. See Lesson 16 for more information.

To enter a number

1. Select the cell into which you want to enter a number by clicking the cell.

2. Type the number. To enter a negative number, precede it with a minus sign, or surround it with parentheses.

3. Click on the Enter button on the formula bar, or press Enter.

 ####### If you enter a number, and it appears in the cell as all number signs (#######) or scientific notation (for example, 7.78E+06), don't worry—the number is okay. The cell is not wide enough to display the number. For a quick fix, select the cell, and choose Format Column AutoFit Selection. For more information, see Lesson 19.

ENTERING DATES AND TIMES

You can enter dates and times in a variety of formats. When you enter a date using a format shown in Table 4.1, Excel converts the date into a number which represents the number of days since January 1, 1900. Although you won't see this number (Excel displays it as a normal date), the number is used whenever a calculation involves a date. This feature is called AutoFormat.

TABLE 4.1 VALID FORMATS FOR DATES AND TIMES

FORMAT	EXAMPLE
MM/DD/YY	4/8/58 or 04/08/58
MMM–YY	Jan–92
DD–MMM–YY	28–Oct–91
DD–MMM	6–Sep
HH:MM	16:50
HH:MM:SS	8:22:59
HH:MM AM/PM	7:45 PM
HH:MM:SS AM/PM	11:45:16 AM
MM/DD/YY HH:MM	11/8/80 4:20
HH:MM MM/DD/YY	4:20 11/18/80

To enter a date or time

1. Select the cell into which you want to enter a date or time.

2. Type the date or time in the format in which you want it displayed.

3. Click on the Enter button on the formula bar, or press Enter.

 Day or Night?   Unless you type AM or PM, Excel assumes that you are using a 24-hour military clock. Therefore, 8:20 is assumed to be AM, not PM. If you type 8:20PM, Excel displays the military time equivalent: 20:20 in the formula bar.

ENTERING DATA QUICKLY

Excel offers several features for helping you copy entries into several cells at the same time. For example, you might want to avoid typing the same data over and over.

- To copy an existing entry into several surrounding cells, you can use the Fill feature.

- To have Excel insert a sequence of entries in neighboring cells (for example Monday, Tuesday, Wednesday), you can use AutoFill.

- To have Excel calculate and insert a series of entries according to your specifications (for example 5, 10, 15, 20), you can fill with a series.

- To have Excel complete an entry for you according to the entries you've already made in that column.

These features are explained in greater detail in the following sections.

COPYING ENTRIES WITH FILL

You can copy an existing entry into any surrounding cells, by performing the following steps:

1. Select the cell whose contents you want to copy.

2. Position the mouse pointer over the selected cell, and click and drag it over all the cells into which you want to copy the cell entry.

3. Open the Edit menu, and select Fill. The Fill submenu appears.

4. Select the direction in which you want to copy the entry. For example, if you choose Right, Excel inserts the entry into the selected cells to the right.

An easier way to fill is to drag the fill handle in the lower right corner of the selected cell to highlight the cells into which you want to copy the entry (see Figure 4.2). When you release the mouse button, the contents of the original cell are copied to the selected cells.

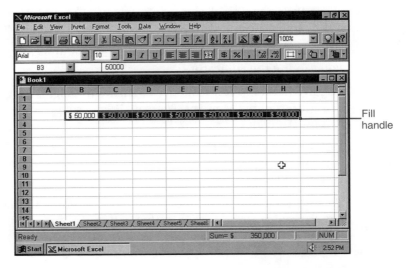

Fill handle

FIGURE 4.2   Drag the fill handle to copy the contents and formatting into neighboring cells.

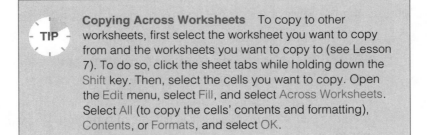

TIP   **Copying Across Worksheets**   To copy to other worksheets, first select the worksheet you want to copy from and the worksheets you want to copy to (see Lesson 7). To do so, click the sheet tabs while holding down the Shift key. Then, select the cells you want to copy. Open the Edit menu, select Fill, and select Across Worksheets. Select All (to copy the cells' contents and formatting), Contents, or Formats, and select OK.

SMART COPYING WITH AUTOFILL

Unlike Fill, which merely copies an entry to one or more cells, AutoFill copies intelligently. For example, if you want to enter the days of the week (Monday through Sunday), you type the first entry (Monday), and AutoFill inserts the others for you. Try it:

1. Type **Monday** into a cell.

2. Drag the fill handle up, down, left, or right to select six more cells.

3. Release the mouse button. Excel inserts the remaining days of the week, in order, into the selected cells.

Excel has the days of the week stored as an AutoFill entry. You can store your own series as AutoFill entries. Here's how you do it:

1. Open the Tools menu, and choose Options. The Options dialog box appears.

2. Click on the Custom Lists tab. The selected tab moves up front, as shown in Figure 4.3.

3. Click on the Add button. An insertion point appears in the List Entries text box.

4. Type the entries you want to use for your AutoFill entries (for example, **Q1, Q2, Q3, Q4**). Press Enter at the end of each entry.

5. Click on the OK button.

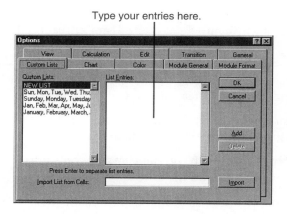

FIGURE 4.3   Excel lets you create your own AutoFill series.

Now that you have your own AutoFill entry, you can type any item in the list and use AutoFill to insert the remaining entries.

ENTERING A SERIES WITH AUTOFILL

Although AutoFill is good for a brief series of entries, you may encounter situations in which you need more control or need to fill lots of cells with incremental entries. In such situations, you should use the series feature. Excel recognizes four types of series, shown in Table 4.2.

TABLE 4.2   DATA SERIES

SERIES	INITIAL ENTRY	RESULTING SERIES
Linear	1, 2	3, 4, 5
	100, 99	98, 97, 96
	1, 3	5, 7, 9
Growth	10, 20	40, 80, 160
	10, 50	250, 1250, 6250
Date	Mon	Tue, Wed, Thur
	Feb	Mar, Apr, May
	Qtr1	Qtr2, Qtr3, Qtr4
Autofill	Team 1	Team 2, Team 3, Team 4
	Qtr 4	Qtr 1, Qtr 2, Qtr 3

Here's what you do to create a series:

1. Enter a value in one cell and press Enter. This value will be the starting or ending value in the series.

2. Select the cells with the value and the cells into which you want to extend the series.

3. Pull down the Edit menu, select Fill, and select Series. The Series dialog box, shown in Figure 4.4, appears.

4. Under Series in, select Rows or Columns. This tells Excel whether to fill down a column or across a row.

5. Under Type, choose a series type (refer to Table 4.2.).

6. Adjust the Step value (the amount between each series value), and Stop value (the last value you want Excel to enter), if necessary.

7. Click on OK, or press Enter, and the series is created.

FIGURE 4.4   The Series dialog box.

ENTERING DATA WITH AUTOCOMPLETE

When you type the first few letters of an entry, AutoComplete intelligently completes the entry for you, based on entries you've already made. AutoComplete works with data entered in columns only, not rows. For example, if you want to enter a column of countries (England, Spain, Italy), you type all the entries once, and the next time you type one of these entries, AutoComplete inserts it for you. Try it:

1. Type **England** into a cell. Press Enter. Type **Spain**; press Enter. Then type **Italy** and press Enter.

2. Type **e.** England appears in the cell. Then press **Enter** to move down to the next cell. Type **i.** Italy appears in the cell. Press Enter to move down to the next cell. Then type **s.** Excel inserts the rest of each entry for you.

3. To see a list of possible cell entries on your worksheet, right-click a cell to display the shortcut menu. Choose Pick From List. Excel shows you a PickList (in alphabetical order) that was automatically created from the words you typed in the column.

4. Click a word in the PickList to insert an entry.

In this lesson, you learned how to enter different types of data and how to automate data entry. In the next lesson, you will learn how to edit entries.

Editing
Entries

In this lesson, you will learn how to make changes to entries in an Excel worksheet and undo those changes.

Editing Data

After you enter data into a cell, you may change it. In Excel, you can edit cell text in either the formula bar or in the cell.

To edit an entry, do this:

1. Select the cell in which you want to edit data.

2. Position the insertion point in the formula bar with the mouse, or press F2, or double-click on the cell. This puts you in Edit mode; Edit appears in the status bar.

3. Press ← or → to move the insertion point. Use the Backspace key to delete characters to the left, or the Delete key to delete characters to the right. Then type any characters you want to add.

4. Click on the Enter button on the formula bar, or press Enter to accept your changes.

Checking Your Spelling

Excel offers a spell checking feature that rapidly finds and highlights the misspellings in a worksheet.

To run the spell checker

1. Open the Tools menu and select Spelling. Excel finds the first misspelled word and displays it at the top of the

Spelling dialog box. Excel's estimate of the correct word appears in the Change To box and in the suggestions list. See Figure 5.1.

2. If a suggestion is correct, click on the word in the Suggestions list (if necessary), and then click Change to change the misspelled word. Or click Change All to change all occurrences of the misspelled word. If desired, you can click Add to add the word to the custom dictionary.

3. If a suggestion is wrong, you can do any of the following:

   • Click Suggest to display words in the Suggestions list.

   • Click the Ignore to leave the word unchanged.

   • Click Ignore All to leave all occurrences of the word unchanged.

   • Or type your own word in the Change To box if Spelling cannot come up with the right one.

4. When the spell checker doesn't find any more misspelled words, it displays a prompt telling you that spell check is complete. Click OK to confirm.

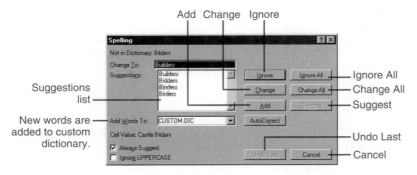

FIGURE 5.1 Correct spelling mistakes with the Spell options in the Spelling dialog box.

Choose the Wrong Option?   If you select the wrong Spell option, you can click the Undo Last button in the Spelling dialog box to undo the last option you chose or correct the mistake after you exit the spell checker. Exit Spelling at any time by clicking Cancel.

USING AUTOCORRECT

Excel's new AutoCorrect feature automatically corrects common typing mistakes as you type. When you press Enter, Excel enters the corrected text in the cell.

With AutoCorrect, you can correct two initial capitals. For example, if you type **MAine** and press Enter, Excel will enter Maine in the cell. AutoCorrect capitalizes the names of days. You can also replace text as you type. For example, if you always type **breif** instead of brief, you can add these entries to the AutoCorrect list and AutoCorrect will fix it for you.

To add entries to the AutoCorrect list, do this:

1. Open the Tools menu and select AutoCorrect. The AutoCorrect dialog box appears, as shown in Figure 5.2.

2. If you want to turn off an AutoCorrect option, click a check box next to the option. The check mark is removed from the check box, indicating the option is turned off.

3. To add an entry to the AutoCorrect list, type the text you want to replace in the Replace text box. Press Tab to move the insertion point to the With text box. Type the replacement text in the With text box.

4. Click the Add button. This will add the entry to the AutoCorrect list.

5. If you want to delete an entry from the AutoCorrect list, use the scroll bar to move to the entry in the list that you want to delete. Click on the entry. Then click the Delete button.

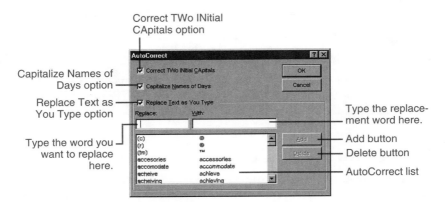

Correct TWo INitial CApitals option

Capitalize Names of Days option

Replace Text as You Type option

Type the word you want to replace here.

Type the replacement word here.

Add button

Delete button

AutoCorrect list

FIGURE 5.2   Add entries to the AutoCorrect list to correct common typographical errors as you work.

UNDOING AN ACTION

You can undo almost anything in a worksheet. To undo a change, do one of the following:

- Open the Edit menu, and choose Undo.
- Press Ctrl+Z.

 • Click on the Undo button in the Standard toolbar.

To undo an Undo (reverse a change), take one of these actions:

- Open the Edit menu, and select Redo.

 • Click on the Repeat button in the Standard toolbar.

 Undo/Repeat One Act   The Undo and Repeat features only undo or repeat the most recent action you took.

FINDING AND REPLACING DATA

With Excel's Find and Replace features, you can locate data and then replace the original data with new data. When you have a label, a value, or formula that is entered incorrectly throughout the worksheet, you can use the Edit Replace command to search and replace all occurrences with the correct data.

To find and replace data, follow these steps:

1. Select the cells that contain the data you want to search. (See Lesson 10 for more information on selecting cells.)

2. Open the Edit menu and select Replace. The Replace dialog box appears, as shown in Figure 5.3.

3. Type the text you want to find and replace in the Find What text box.

4. Click in the Replace With text box or press the Tab key. Type the text you want to use as the replacement in the Replace With text box.

5. Click the Replace All button to begin the search and re- place all occurrences of the data you specified. When Excel finishes replacing all occurrences, click outside the selected cells to deselect them.

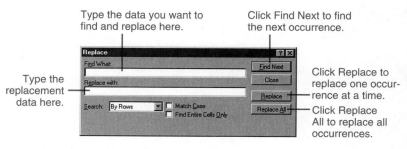

Type the data you want to find and replace here.

Click Find Next to find the next occurrence.

Type the replacement data here.

Click Replace to replace one occur- rence at a time.

Click Replace All to replace all occurrences.

FIGURE 5.3   Find and replace data with the Replace dialog box.

Replace One at a Time   Be sure you want to replace all occurrences before you select the Replace All button. You can also search for and replace one occurrence at a time. To do this, click the Find Next button to find the next occurrence of the data. Then click the Replace button or click the Find Next button again to skip the occurrence.

ADDING NOTES TO CELLS

Cell notes can provide detailed information about data used in a worksheet. Once you create a note, you can display the note you've added to the cell(s). The cell note that displays on the worksheet is called a CellTip.

To add a note to a cell, do the following:

1. Select the cell to which you want to add a note.

2. Open the Insert menu and choose Note. The Cell Note dialog box appears.

3. Type the note in the space provided under Text Note.

4. Click OK to add the note to the cell.

To view a CellTip, point to a cell that contains a red dot in its upper right corner. Excel displays the CellTip on the worksheet, as shown in Figure 5.4.

Move the mouse pointer to this cell
with the red dot to display the CellTip.   CellTip

	A	B	C	D	E	F	G	H	I
1		Sandy Shores Sales Report							
2									
3		Q1	Q2	Q3	Q4	Total			
4	East	100	100	100	100	400			
5	West	100	100	100	100	Includes			
6	North	200	200	200	200	Accounting			
7	South	200	200	200	200	Department			
8						expenses			
9									
10									
11									
12									
13									
14									
15									
16									

Sheet1 / Sheet2 / Sheet3 / Sheet4 / Sheet5 / Sheet6 /

FIGURE 5.4   Viewing a CellTip in a worksheet.

CellTips   Excel's new CellTips feature allows you to display a cell note on the worksheet by simply moving the mouse pointer to the red dot in a cell.

To edit a note, select the cell that contains the note, and choose Insert Note. In the Note dialog box, click on the note name in the Notes in Sheet list, and make your changes in the Text Note box. To delete a note, click on the note name in the Notes in Sheet list, and click Delete.

In this lesson, you learned how to edit cell data, undo changes, and add notes to cells. In the next lesson, you will learn how to work with workbook files.

6

WORKING WITH WORKBOOK FILES

In this lesson you will learn how to save, close, and open workbook files, and how to create new workbooks. You will also learn how to locate misplaced files.

SAVING AND NAMING A WORKBOOK

Whatever you type into a workbook is stored only in your computer's temporary memory. If you exit Excel, that data will be lost, so it is important to save your workbook files regularly.

The first time you save a workbook to disk, you have to name it. Here's how you do it:

1. Open the File menu, and select Save, or click on the Save button in the Standard toolbar. The Save As dialog box appears as shown in Figure 6.1.

2. Type the name you want to give the workbook in the File Name text box. You may use any combination of letters or numbers up to 218 characters including spaces and the complete path (drive letter, server name, and folder path), such as **C:\MY DOCUMENTS\1996 BUDGET**.

3. To save the file to a different folder, double-click on that folder in the files and folders list. (You can move up a folder level by clicking on the Up One Level button on the Save toolbar at the top of the dialog box. After you move up a folder level, you can move back down by selecting a drive in the Save In box and navigating the files and folder list.) When you save a file to any of the places listed in the Save In box, here's what happens:

- **Desktop**   Saves the file as an icon on the Windows desktop. Double-click on the icon on your desktop to quickly start Excel and open the workbook file. If you're working on a project in Excel on a daily basis, you might want to have the file icon on the desktop.

- **My Computer**   Saves the file to Windows' My Computer. Open the My Computer window and double-click on the file icon to start Excel and open the workbook file. If you are working in My Computer regularly, it might be convenient to save the file to My Computer. You can also save your file to your hard drive, floppy drive, or CD in My Computer.

- **Network Neighborhood**   Saves the file to Windows' Network Neighborhood. Open Network Neighborhood and double-click on the file icon to start Excel and open the workbook file. If you work in Network Neighborhood regularly, save the file to Network Neighborhood.

4. To save the file on a different drive, click on the arrow to the right of the Save In box, and click on the drive.

5. Click the Save button, or press Enter.

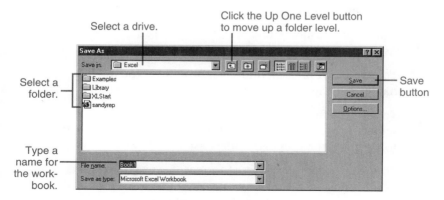

FIGURE 6.1   The Save As dialog box.

> **Default Directory**   You can set up a default directory where Excel will save all your workbook files. Open the Tools menu, and select Options. Click on the General tab. Click inside the Default File Location text box, and type a complete path to the drive and directory you want to use (the directory must be an existing one). Select OK.

To save a file you have already saved, simply click on the Save button, or press Ctrl+S. Or open the File menu, and select Save. Excel automatically saves the workbook without displaying the Save As dialog box.

> **Control Menu Shortcut**   In Excel for Windows 95, you can right-click on the Control Menu and display a shortcut menu. This menu contains some of the commands you'll use most frequently with your workbook files.

SAVING A WORKBOOK UNDER A NEW NAME

Sometimes, you may want to change a workbook but keep a copy of the original workbook, or you may want to create a new workbook by modifying an existing one. You can do this by saving the workbook under another name or in another folder. Here's how:

1. Open the File menu, and select Save As. You get the Save As dialog box.

2. To save the workbook under a new name, type the new name over the existing one in the File Name text box.

3. To save the file on a different drive or in a different folder, select the drive letter from the Save In box and the folder from the files and folders list.

4. To save the file in a different format (for example, Lotus 1-2-3), click on the arrow to the right of the Save as Type drop-down list, and select the desired format.

5. Click the Save button, or press Enter.

Backup Files You can have Excel create a backup copy of each workbook file you save. Click on the Options button in the Save As dialog box, select Always Create Backup, and click on OK. To use the backup file, choose File Open, and select Backup Files from the Files of Type list. Double-click on the backup file to open the file.

CREATING A NEW WORKBOOK

You can create a new workbook by modifying an existing one or by opening a blank workbook and starting from scratch. Here's how you open a blank workbook:

1. Pull down the File menu, and select New or press Ctrl+N. The New dialog box appears, as shown in Figure 6.2. This dialog box contains two tabs: General and Spreadsheet Solutions.

2. The Workbook icon in the General options should be selected. If not, click on the Workbook icon.

3. Click on OK, or press Enter. A new workbook opens on-screen with a default name in the title bar.

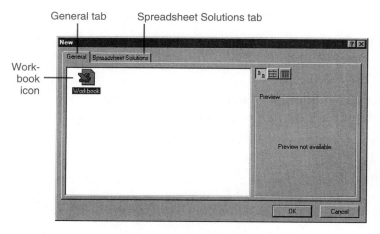

FIGURE 6.2   The General tab in the New dialog box.

New Workbook   The New Workbook feature in Excel for Windows 95 and Excel 5 are similar. The New dialog box in Excel for Windows 95 has two tabs: General and Spreadsheet Solutions. The General option lets you create a new workbook. The new Spreadsheet Solutions option lets you create a new workbook based on a template. See Lesson 21 for more information. In Excel 5, the New dialog box contains a list of new workbook options such as Workbook and Slides.

CLOSING WORKBOOKS

Closing a workbook removes its workbook window from the screen. To close a workbook, do this:

1. If the window you want to close isn't currently active, make it so by selecting the workbook from the list of workbooks at the bottom of the Window menu.

2. Click the right mouse button on the workbook's Control Menu and select Close from the shortcut menu. If you have not yet saved the workbook, you will be prompted to do so.

OPENING AN EXISTING WORKBOOK

If you have closed a workbook and then later you want to use it again, you must open it. Here's how you do it:

1. Pull down the File menu, and select Open, or click on the Open button in the Standard toolbar. The Open dialog box appears, as shown in Figure 6.3.

2. If the file is not on the current drive, click on the arrow to the right of the Look In box, and select the correct drive.

3. If the file is not in the current folder, select the correct folder from the files and folders list.

4. Do one of the following:

- Choose a file from the files and folders list.

- Type the name of the file in the File Name box. As you type, Excel highlights the first file name in the list that matches your entry.

5. Click on Open, or press Enter.

Type the file   ...or select the
name...   file from the list.

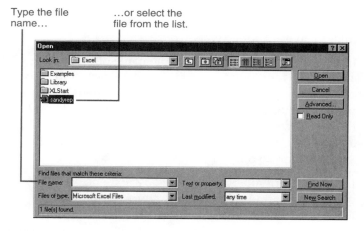

FIGURE 6.3   The Open dialog box.

Preview Workbook Before Opening It   Before you open a workbook in Excel for Windows 95, you can preview the contents of the workbook. Click the Preview button in the Open toolbar at the top of the Open dialog box. Excel displays the contents of the workbook in a window on the right side of the dialog box.

FINDING A WORKBOOK FILE

If you forgot where you saved a file, Excel can help you with its new Search for Files option in the Open dialog box. Here's what you do to have Excel hunt for a file:

1. Open the File menu, and select Open, or click on the Open button in the Standard tool bar. You'll get the Open dialog box, as shown in Figure 6.4.

2. In the Look In box, click the drive you want to search. For example, if you select [C:], Excel will search the C drive. If you select [C:] and then the Excel folder, Excel searches only the EXCEL directory on drive C. You can select My Computer to search all drives on your computer.

3. If desired, in the files and folders list, double-click on the folder you want to search.

4. In the File Name text box, type the name of the file you are looking for. You can use wild-card characters in place of characters you can't remember. Use an asterisk (*) in place of a group of characters, or use a question mark (?) in place of a single character. For example, **sales??** finds all files that begin with the word "sales," such as SALES01, SALES02, and so on.

5. In the Text or Property box, type any text enclosed in quotations to find the workbook based on specific text. For example, type **brook trout** to find the workbook that contains the words "brook trout." Choose an option from the Last Modified box to specify a time period.

6. To have Excel search all subfolders of the drive you specify, click the Commands and Settings button on the Open toolbar and choose Search Subfolders from the menu.

7. The New Search button clears out anything you may have typed in the File Name, Text or Property, and Last Modified text boxes.

8. Click on the Find Now button. Excel finds the files that match the search instructions you entered, and displays them in the files and folders list.

9. Look through the list, highlight the file you want, and click on the Open button.

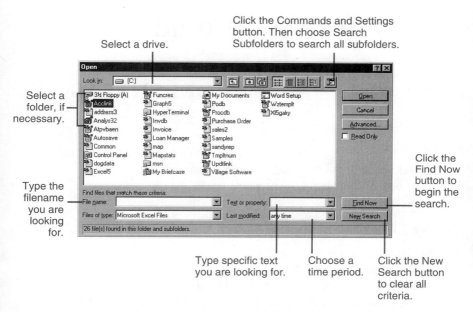

FIGURE 6.4 The Search options in the Open dialog box ask you to specify what you want to search for.

MOVING AMONG OPEN WORKBOOKS

Sometimes, you may have more than one workbook open at a time. There are several ways to move among open workbooks:

- If part of the workbook window is visible, click on it.
- Open the Window menu, and select the name of the workbook you want to go to.
- Press Ctrl+F6 to move from one workbook window to another.

In this lesson, you learned how to save, close, and open workbooks, as well as find misplaced workbook files. The next lesson teaches you how to work with the worksheets in a workbook.

LESSON 7

WORKING WITH WORKSHEETS

This lesson teaches you how to add worksheets to and delete worksheets from workbooks. You will also learn how to copy, move, and rename worksheets.

SELECTING WORKSHEETS

By default, each workbook consists of 16 worksheet pages whose names appear on tabs near the bottom of the screen. You can insert new worksheet pages or delete worksheet pages as desired. One advantage to having multiple worksheet pages is that you can copy and move worksheets within a workbook or from one workbook to another. Another advantage is that you can keep separate pages of data more organized.

Before we get into the details of inserting, deleting, and copying worksheets, you should know how to select one or more worksheets. Here's what you need to know:

- To select a single worksheet, click on its tab.

- To select several neighboring worksheets, click on the tab of the first worksheet in the group, and then hold down the Shift key while clicking on the tab of the last worksheet in the group.

- To select several non-neighboring worksheets, hold down the Ctrl key while clicking on each worksheet's tab.

- If you select two or more worksheets, they remain selected until you ungroup them. To ungroup worksheets, do one of the following:

- Right-click on one of the selected worksheets, and choose Ungroup Sheets.

- Hold down the Shift key while clicking on the active tab.

- Click on any tab outside the group.

INSERTING WORKSHEETS

To insert a new worksheet, perform the following steps:

1. Select the worksheet before which you want the new worksheet inserted. For example, if you select Sheet4, the new worksheet (which will be called Sheet17 because the workbook already contains 16 worksheets) will be inserted before Sheet4.

2. Open the Insert menu.

3. Select Worksheet. Excel inserts the new worksheet, as shown in Figure 7.1.

Worksheet inserted before Sheet 4.

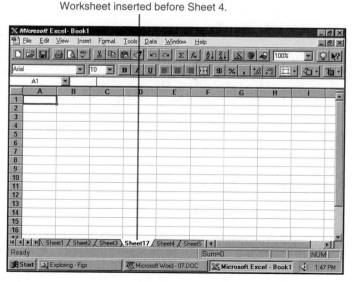

FIGURE 7.1 Excel inserts the new worksheet.

DELETING WORKSHEETS

If you plan on using only one worksheet, you can remove the 15 other worksheets to free up memory. Here's how you remove a worksheet:

1. Select the worksheet(s) you want to delete.

2. Open the Edit menu.

3. Click on Delete Sheet. A dialog box appears, asking you to confirm the deletion.

4. Click on the OK button. The worksheets are deleted.

MOVING AND COPYING WORKSHEETS

You can move or copy worksheets within a workbook or from one workbook to another. Here's how:

1. Select the worksheet(s) you want to move or copy. If you want to move or copy worksheets from one workbook to another, be sure to open the target workbook.

2. Open the Edit menu, and choose Move or Copy Sheet. The Move or Copy dialog box appears, as shown in Figure 7.2.

3. To move the worksheet(s) to a different workbook, select the workbook's name from the To Book drop-down list. If you want to move or copy the worksheet(s) to a new workbook, select [new book] in the To Book drop-down list. Excel will create a new workbook and then copy or move the worksheet(s) to it.

4. In the Before Sheet list box, choose the worksheet before which you want the selected worksheet(s) to be moved.

5. To copy the selected worksheet(s), select Create a Copy.

6. Select OK. The selected worksheet(s) are copied or moved, as specified.

MOVING WITHIN A WORKBOOK BY DRAGGING AND DROPPING

An easier way to copy or move worksheets within a workbook is to use the Drag & Drop feature. First, select the tab of the worksheet(s) you want to copy or move. Move the mouse pointer over one of the selected tabs, click and hold the mouse button, and drag the tab where you want it moved. To copy the worksheet, hold down the Ctrl key while dragging. When you release the mouse button, the worksheet is copied or moved.

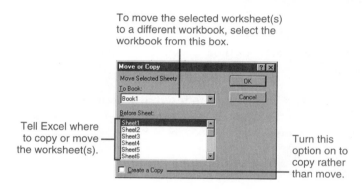

To move the selected worksheet(s) to a different workbook, select the workbook from this box.

Tell Excel where to copy or move the worksheet(s).

Turn this option on to copy rather than move.

FIGURE 7.2   The Move or Copy dialog box asks you where you want to copy or move a worksheet.

MOVING BETWEEN WORKBOOKS BY DRAGGING AND DROPPING

You can also use the Drag and Drop feature to quickly copy or move worksheets between workbooks. First, open the workbooks you want to use for the copy or move. Choose Window Arrange and select the Tiled option. Click on OK to arrange the windows so that a small portion of each one appears on-screen. Select the tab of the worksheet(s) you want to copy or move. Move the mouse pointer over one of the selected tabs, click and hold the mouse button, and drag the tab where you want it moved. To copy the worksheet, hold down the Ctrl key while dragging. When you release the mouse button, the worksheet is copied or moved.

CHANGING THE WORKSHEET TAB NAMES

By default, all worksheets are named Sheet and are numbered starting with the number 1. So that you'll have a better idea of the information each sheet contains, you can change the names that appear on the tabs. Here's how you do it:

1. Select the worksheet whose name you want to change.

2. Right-click on the tab and select Rename from the short-cut menu. Or double-click on the worksheet's tab. Excel shows you the Rename Sheet dialog box.

3. Type a new name for the worksheet, and click on the OK button.

In this lesson, you learned how to insert, delete, move, copy, and rename worksheets. In the next lesson, you will learn how to print your workbook.

Printing Your Workbook

In this lesson, you will learn how to print an entire workbook or only a portion of it.

Changing the Page Setup

A workbook is a collection of many worksheets, like pages in a notebook. You can print the whole notebook at once, or just one or more pages at a time.

Before you print a worksheet, you should make sure that the page is set up correctly for printing. Open the File menu and choose Page Setup. You'll see the Page Setup dialog box, as shown in Figure 8.1.

Right-Click on the Workbook Title Bar For quick access to commands that affect a workbook in Excel for Windows 95, right-click on the workbook's title bar, if the workbook appears in a window (not maximized). If the workbook is maximized to a full screen, right-click on the menu bar to access the shortcut menu. For example, to check the page setup, right-click on the title bar or menu bar, and choose Page Setup.

Enter your page setup settings as follows:

Page tab

> **Orientation** Select Portrait to print from left to right across a page or Landscape to print from top to bottom on a page. (Landscape makes the page wider than it is tall.)
>
> **Scaling** You can reduce and enlarge your workbook or force it to fit within a specific page size.

The Margins tab   The Header/Footer tab

The Page tab ————   The Sheet tab

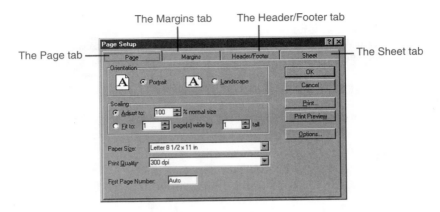

FIGURE 8.1   The Page Setup dialog box.

Paper Size   This is 8 1/2 by 11 inches, by default. You can choose a different size from the list.

Print Quality   You can print a draft of your spreadsheet to print quickly and save wear and tear on your printer, or you can print in high quality for a final copy. Print quality is measured in dpi (dots per inch)—the higher the number, the better the print.

First Page Number   You can set the starting page number to something other than 1. The Auto option (default) tells Excel to set the starting page number to 1 if it is the first page in the print job, or set the first page number at the next sequential number if it is not the first page in the print job.

Margins tab

Top, **Bottom**, **Left**, **Right**   You can adjust the size of the top, bottom, left, and right margins.

From Edge   You can specify how far you want a Header or Footer printed from the edge of the page.

Center on Page   You can center the printing between the left and right margins (horizontally) and between the top and bottom margins (vertically).

Header/Footer tab

Header/Footer You can add a header (such as a title, which repeats at the top of each page) or a footer (such as page numbers, which repeat at the bottom of each page). See Lesson 9 for more information on headers and footers.

Custom Header/Custom Footer You can choose the Custom Header or Custom Footer button to create headers and footers that insert the time, date, worksheet tab name, and workbook file name.

Sheet tab

Print Area You can print a portion of a workbook or worksheet by entering the range of cells you want to print. You can type the range, or drag the Page Setup dialog box out of the way and drag the mouse pointer over the desired cells (see Lesson 9). If you do not select a print area, Excel will print either the sheet or the workbook depending on the options set in the Page tab.

Print Titles If you have a row or column of entries that you want repeated as titles on every page, type the range for this row or column, or drag over the cells with the mouse pointer (see Lesson 9).

Print You can tell Excel exactly how to print some aspects of the workbook. For example, you can have the gridlines (the lines that define the cells) printed. You can also have a color spreadsheet printed in black-and-white.

Page Order You can indicate how data in the worksheet should be read and printed: in sections from top to bottom or in sections from left to right. This is the way Excel handles printing the areas outside the printable area. For example, if some columns to the right don't fit on the first page and some rows don't fit at the bottom of the first page, you can specify which area will print next.

When you are done entering your settings, click on the OK button.

PREVIEWING A PRINT JOB

 After you determine your page setup and print area, you can preview what the printed page will look like before you print. Open the File menu and select Print Preview, or click on the Print Preview button in the Standard toolbar. Your workbook appears as it will when printed.

 TIP A Close-Up View   Zoom in on any area of the preview by clicking on it with the mouse pointer (which looks like a magnifying glass). You can also use the Zoom button at the top of the Print Preview screen.

PRINTING YOUR WORKBOOK

After setting up the page and previewing your data, it is time to print. You can print selected data, selected sheets, or the entire workbook.

To print your workbook:

1. If you want to print a portion of the worksheet, select the range you want to print (see Lesson 10). If you want to print one or more sheets within the workbook, select the sheet tabs. To print the entire workbook, you don't select anything in the workbook.

2. Open the File menu, and select Print (or press Ctrl+P). The Print dialog box appears, as shown in Figure 8.2.

3. Select the options you would like to use:

   Print What   Allows you to print the currently selected cells, the selected worksheets, or the entire workbook.

   Copies   Allows you to print more than one copy of the selection, worksheet, or workbook.

   Collate   Allows you to print a complete copy of the selection, worksheet, or workbook before the first page of the next copy is printed.

Page Range   Lets you print one or more pages. For example, if you want to print only pages 5–10, select Page(s), and then type the numbers of the first and last page you want to print in the From and To boxes.

4. Click on OK, or press Enter.

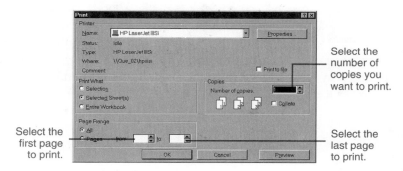

Select the number of copies you want to print.

Select the first page to print.

Select the last page to print.

FIGURE 8.2   The Print dialog box.

While your job is printing, you can continue working in Excel. If the printer is working on another job that you sent, Excel's new Printers folder acts as a print queue and holds the job until the printer is ready for it.

Sometimes you might want to delete a job while it is printing or before it prints. For example, you may think of other numbers to add to the worksheet or realize you forgot to format some text. In such a case, deleting the print job is easy. To display the print queue and delete a print job, follow these steps:

1. Click the Start button and choose Settings.

2. From the Settings menu, choose Printers. The Printers window appears.

3. Double-click the printer icon. The print queue window appears with a list of queued documents. If no documents are waiting to print, there will not be any jobs listed below the column headings.

4. Click on the job you want to delete to select it.

5. Choose Document, Cancel Printing.

 TIP **Clear the Queue!**—To delete all the files from the print queue, choose Printer, Purge Print Jobs from the print queue menu bar.

In this lesson, you learned how to print all or part of your workbook. In the next lesson, you will learn how to print large worksheets.

PRINTING LARGE WORKSHEETS

In this lesson you learn about the many aspects involved in printing a large worksheet.

SELECTING A PRINT AREA

You can tell Excel what part of the worksheet you want to print using the Print Area option of the Page Setup dialog box. This option lets you single out an area as a separate page and then print that page. If the area is too large to fit onto one page, Excel will break it into multiple pages. If you do not select a print area, Excel will print either the sheet or the workbook depending on the options set in the Page tab.

To select a print area

1. Open the File menu and choose Page Setup. The Page Setup dialog box appears.

2. Click the Sheet tab to display the Sheet options.

3. Click in the Print Area text box to display the insertion point. Drag the Page Setup dialog box out of the way and drag the mouse pointer over the desired cells (see Lesson 10), as shown in Figure 9.1. You'll see a dashed line border surrounding the selected area and absolute cell references with $ in the Print Area text box. (If you want to type the range, you don't have to include the $ in the cell references. See Lesson 14 for more information about absolute cell references.)

4. Click Print in the Page Setup dialog box to display the Print dialog box. Then click OK to print your worksheet.

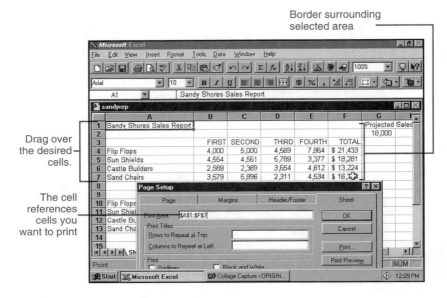

Border surrounding
selected area

Drag over
the desired
cells.

The cell
references
cells you
want to print

Figure 9.1   Selecting a print area.

ADJUSTING PAGE BREAKS

When you print a workbook, Excel determines the page breaks
based on the paper size and margins and the selected print area.
To make the pages look better and break things in logical places,
you may want to override the automatic page breaks. However,
before you add page breaks, try these options:

- Adjust the widths of individual columns to make the best
  use of space (see Lesson 19).

- Consider printing the workbook sideways (using Land-
  scape orientation).

- Change the left, right, top, and bottom margins to
  smaller values.

If after trying these options you still want to insert page breaks, first determine whether you need to limit the number of columns on a page or the number of rows.

To limit the number of columns

1. Select a cell that's in the column to the right of the last column you want on the page. For example, if you want Excel to print only columns A through G on the first page, select a cell in column H.

2. Move to row 1 of that column.

3. Open the Insert menu, and choose Page Break. A dashed line appears to the left of the selected column, showing the position of the page break.

To limit the number of rows

1. Select a cell in the row below the last row you want on the page. For example, if you want Excel to print rows 1 through 12 on the first page, select a cell in row 13.

2. Move to column A of that row.

3. Open the Insert menu, and choose Page Break. A dashed line appears above the selected row.

One Step Page Breaks   You can set the lower right corner of a workbook in one step. Select the cell that is below and to the right of the last cell for the page, and then open the Insert menu, and select Page Break. For example, if you wanted cell G12 to be the last cell on that page, move to cell H13, and set the page break.

Remove a Page Break   To remove a page break, move to the cell that you used to set the page break, open the Insert menu, and choose Remove Page Break.

PRINTING COLUMN AND ROW HEADINGS

Excel provides a way for you to select labels and titles that are located on the top edge and left side of your large worksheet, and print them on every page of the printout. This option is useful when a worksheet is too wide to print on a single page. The extra columns will be printed on subsequent pages without any descriptive information unless you use the Repeat Rows at Top and Repeat Columns at Left options in the Page Setup dialog box.

When you specify the column and row headings, Excel divides the worksheet into sections, showing dashed borders around the column and row headings you want to repeat. Figure 9.2 shows a worksheet after you specify the column and row headings.

To print column and row headings on every page

1. Open the File menu, and choose Page Setup. The Page Setup dialog box appears.

2. Click the Sheet tab to display the Sheet options.

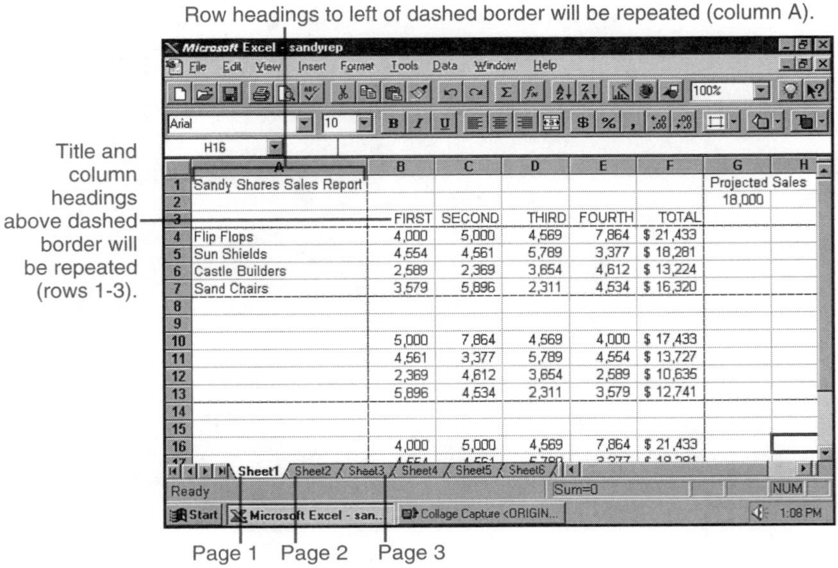

Figure 9.2 Repeating column and row headings on every page.

3. Click in the Rows to Repeat at Top text box to display the insertion point. Then drag the Page Setup dialog box out of the way and drag the mouse pointer over the desired cells (see Lesson 10), as shown in Figure 9.3.

4. Click in the Columns to Repeat at Left text box to display the insertion point. Then drag the dialog box title bar out of the way and drag the mouse pointer over the desired cells (see Lesson 10), as shown in Figure 9.3.

5. Click OK to close the Page Setup dialog box and see the results in your worksheet or click Print to see the Print dialog box and print your worksheet.

Remove the Rows and Columns You Want to Repeat To remove the rows and columns you want to repeat, delete the cell coordinates in the Rows to Repeat at Top and Columns to Repeat at Left text boxes.

Drag over the row headings you want to repeat.

Drag over the column headings you want to repeat.

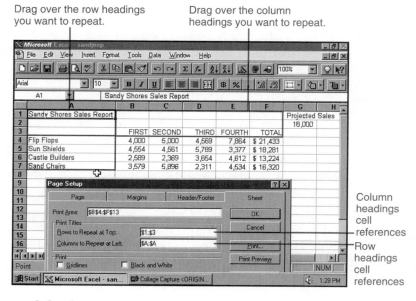

Figure 9.3 Specifying column and row headings with Sheet Options.

ADDING HEADERS AND FOOTERS

Excel lets you add headers and footers to print information at the top and bottom of every page of the printout. The information can include any text, page numbers, the current date and time, the workbook file name, and the worksheet tab name.

You can choose the headers and footers suggested by Excel, or you can include any text plus special commands to control the appearance of the header or footer. For example, you can apply bold, italic, or underline to the header or footer text (see Lesson 17). You can also left-align, center, or right-align your text in a header or footer (see Lesson 16).

To add headers and footers

1. Open the File menu and choose Page Setup. The Page Setup dialog box appears.

2. Click the Header/Footer tab to display the Header and Footer options, as shown in Figure 9.4. Notice that by default Excel uses the name of the sheet as the header and Page 1 as the footer.

3. To select a different header, click the drop-down arrow next to the Header text box. You'll see a list of suggested header information. Scroll through the list and click on a header you want. The sample header appears at the top of the Header/Footer tab.

4. To select a different footer, click the drop-down arrow next to the Footer text box. You'll see a list of suggested footer information. Scroll through the list and click on a footer you want. The sample footer appears at the bottom of the Header/Footer tab.

5. Click OK to close the Page Setup dialog box and return to your worksheet or click the Print button to display the Print dialog box. Then click OK to print your worksheet.

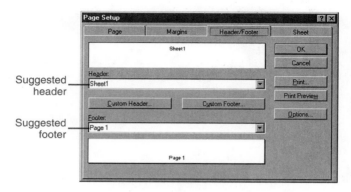

Suggested header ——

Suggested footer ——

Figure 9.4 Adding headers and footers with Header/Footer options.

In this lesson, you learned how to print a large worksheet. In the next lesson, you will learn how to work with ranges.

10

WORKING WITH RANGES

In this lesson, you will learn how to select and name cell ranges.

WHAT IS A RANGE?

A *range* is a rectangular group of connected cells. The cells in a range may all be in a column, or a row, or any combination of columns and rows, as long as the range forms a rectangle, as shown in Figure 10.1.

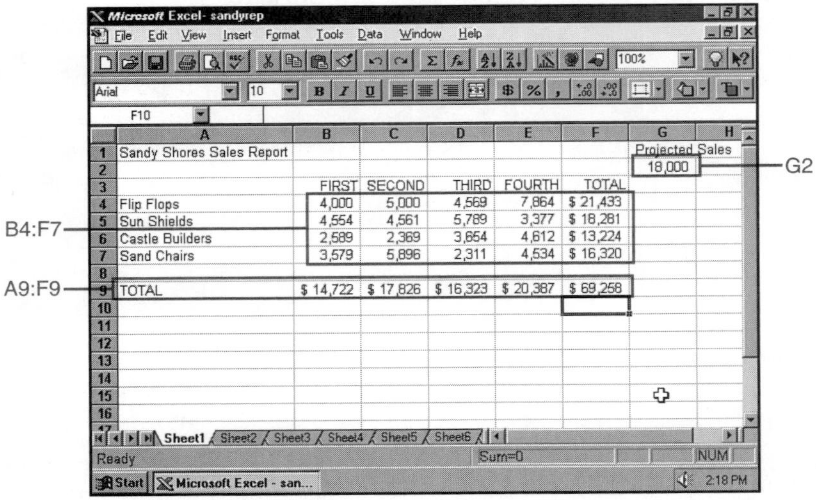

FIGURE 10.1 A range is any combination of cells that forms a rectangle.

Learning how to use ranges can save you time. For example, you can select a range and use it to format a group of cells with one step.

Ranges are referred to by their anchor points (the top left corner and the lower right corner). For example, the ranges shown in Figure 10.1 are B4:F7, A9:F9, and G2.

SELECTING A RANGE

To select a range, use the mouse:

1. Move the pointer to the upper left corner of a range.

2. Click and hold the left mouse button.

3. Drag the mouse to the lower right corner of the range and release the mouse button.

4. To select the same range of cells on more than one worksheet, select the worksheets (see Lesson 7).

5. Release the mouse button. The selected range will be highlighted.

There are various techniques you can use to select a range on a worksheet. You can select cells that are next to each other, and you can select noncontiguous ranges (ranges that aren't next to each other). You can also select an entire row, column, or worksheet with one click. The selecting techniques are shown in Table 10.1.

TABLE 10.1 SELECTING TECHNIQUES

SELECTION	TECHNIQUE
Cell	Click the cell you want to select.
Range	Click the first cell in the range. Hold down the left mouse button and drag across the cells you want to include.
Noncontiguous ranges	Select the first range. Hold down the Ctrl key and select the next range.

continues

TABLE 10.1   CONTINUED

SELECTION	TECHNIQUE
Row	Click on the row heading number at the left edge of the worksheet. You also can press Shift+Spacebar.
Column	Click on the column heading letter at the top edge of the worksheet. You also can press Ctrl+Spacebar.
Entire worksheet	Click the Select All button (the blank rectangle in the upper left corner of the worksheet above row 1 and left of column A). You also can press Ctrl+A.
Range that is out of view	Press F5 (Goto) and type the range address in the Reference text box. For example, to move to cell Z50, type Z50 and press Enter. To select the range R100 to T250, type R100:T250 and press Enter.

NAMING CELLS AND CELL RANGES

Up to this point, you have used cell addresses to refer to cells. Although that works, it is often more convenient to name cells with more recognizable names. For example, say you want to determine your net income by subtracting expenses from income (see Lesson 13). You can name the cell that contains your total income INCOME, and name the cell that contains your total expenses EXPENSES. You can then determine your net income by using the formula:

=INCOME–EXPENSES

Naming cells and ranges also makes it easier to cut, copy, and move blocks of cells, as explained in Lesson 11.

To name a cell range:

1. Select the range of cells you want to name. Make sure all the cells are on the same worksheet. (You can't name cells and ranges that are located on more than one sheet.)

2. Click inside the name box. See Figure 10.2.

3. Type a range name (up to 255 characters). Valid names can include letters, numbers, periods, and underlines, but no spaces. Also, a number cannot be the first character in the range name.

4. Press Enter.

5. To see the list of range names, click the down arrow next to the Name box on the formula bar.

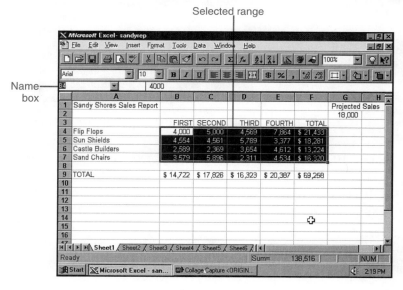

FIGURE 10.2   Type a name in the name box.

Another way to name a range is to select it and then open the Insert menu, and select Name, Define. This displays the Define Name dialog box, shown in Figure 10.3. Type a name in the Names in Workbook text box, and click on OK.

The Define Name dialog box allows you to see what range a range name contains. Click on a range name in the Names in Workbook list. You'll see the cell address(es) assigned to the range name in the Refers To text box.

The dollar signs in the cell addresses indicate absolute cell references, which always refer to the same cell. An absolute cell reference will not be adjusted if changes are made to those cells in the worksheet (see Lesson 14).

To delete a range name, click on a name in the Names in Workbook list, click on the Delete button.

Type a name here. ———

Selected range appears here. You can edit the range or type a new one.

FIGURE 10.3   The Define Name dialog box.

In this lesson, you learned how to select and name ranges. In the next lesson, you will learn how to copy, move, and erase data.

COPYING, MOVING, AND ERASING DATA

LESSON 11

In this lesson, you will learn to organize your worksheet to meet your changing needs by copying, moving, and erasing data.

When you copy or move data, a copy of that data is placed in a temporary storage area called the *Clipboard*.

What Is the Clipboard? The Clipboard is an area of memory that is accessible to all Windows programs. The Clipboard is used by all Windows programs to copy or move data from place to place within a program, or between programs.

COPYING DATA

You make copies of data to use in other sections of your worksheet or in other worksheets or workbooks. The original data remains in place, and a copy of it is placed where you indicate.

To copy data

1. Select the range or cell that you want to copy.

2. Pull down the Edit menu, and select Copy, or press Ctrl+C. The contents of the selected cell(s) are copied to the Clipboard.

3. Select the first cell in the area where you would like to place the copy. (To copy the data to another worksheet or workbook, change to that worksheet or workbook.)

4. Pull down the Edit menu, and choose Paste, or press
Ctrl+V.

You can copy the same data to several places in the worksheet by
repeating the Edit Paste command. Data copied to the Clipboard
remains there until you copy or cut something else.

Quick Copying with Drag and Drop   The fastest way to
copy is to use the Drag and Drop feature. Select the cells
you want to copy, and then hold down the Ctrl key while
dragging the cell selector border where you want the cells
copied (see Figure 11.1). When you release the mouse
button, the contents are copied to the new location. If you
forget to hold down the Ctrl key, Excel moves the data
rather than copying it.

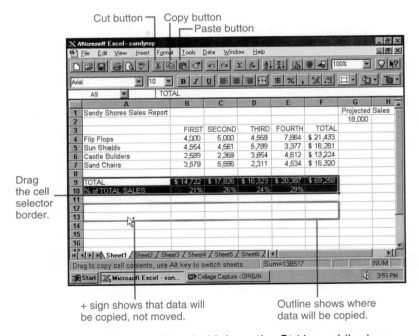

Figure 11.1   To copy data, hold down the Ctrl key while dragging the cell selector border.

MOVING DATA

Moving data is similar to copying, except that the data is removed from its original place and moved to the new location.

To move data

1. Select the range or cell that you want to move.

2. Pull down the Edit menu, and select Cut, or press Ctrl+X.

3. Select the first cell in the area where you would like to place the data. To move the data to another worksheet, change to that worksheet.

4. Pull down the Edit menu, and select Paste, or press Ctrl+V.

To move data quickly, use the Drag and Drop feature. Select the data to be moved, and then drag the cell selector border without holding down the Ctrl key.

Shortcut Menu   When cutting, copying, and pasting data, don't forget the shortcut menu. Simply select the cells you want to cut or copy, right-click on the selected cells, and choose the appropriate command from the shortcut menu that appears.

Drag Cells to Move Data between Worksheets   Excel's new Drag Cells Between Worksheets feature lets you move selected ranges between worksheets. To move data to another worksheet in the same workbook, select the range and then hold down the Alt key while dragging the range to the tab for the other worksheet. Continue to drag the range from the sheet tab up to the new location in the worksheet until the range appears where you want it.

ERASING DATA

Although erasing data is fairly easy, you must decide exactly what
you want to erase first. Here are your choices:

- Use the Edit Clear command to erase only the contents or
  formatting of the cells. The Edit Clear command is covered next.

- Use the Edit Delete command to remove the cells and
  everything in them. This is covered in Lesson 12.

  With the Clear command, you can remove the data from
  a cell, or just its formula, formatting, or attached notes.
  Here's what you do:

1. Select the range of cells you wish to clear.

2. Pull down the Edit menu, and choose Clear. The Clear
   submenu appears, as shown in Figure 11.2.

3. Select the desired clear option: All (clears formats, contents, and notes), Formats, Contents, or Notes.

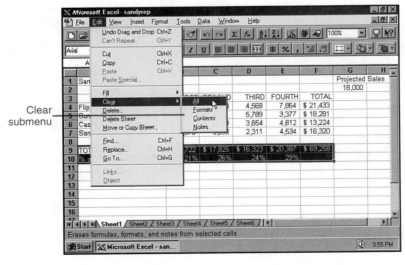

Figure 11.2 Clearing the contents of the selected cells.

Shortcut Menu   When clearing cells, don't forget the shortcut menu. Select the cells you want to clear, right-click on one of them, and then choose Clear Contents.

In this lesson, you learned how to copy and move data. You also learned how to clear data from cells. In the next lesson, you will learn how to insert and delete cells, rows, and columns.

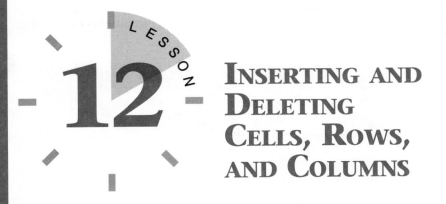

LESSON 12

INSERTING AND DELETING CELLS, ROWS, AND COLUMNS

In this lesson, you will learn how to rearrange your worksheet by adding and deleting cells, rows, and columns.

INSERTING CELLS

Sometimes, you will need to insert information into a worksheet, right in the middle of existing data. With the Insert command, you can insert one or more cells, or entire rows or columns.

Shifting Cells Inserting cells in the middle of existing data will cause those other cells to shift down a row or over a column. If you added formulas to your worksheet that rely on the contents of the shifting cells, this could throw off the calculations (see Lessons 13 and 14). Your formulas are affected when you insert a cell or group of cells. However, formulas adjust automatically when you insert entire rows or entire columns.

To insert a single cell or a group of cells:

1. Select the cell(s) where you want the new cell(s) inserted. Excel will insert the same number of cells as you select.

2. Pull down the Insert menu, and choose Cells. The Insert dialog box shown in Figure 12.1 appears.

3. Select Shift Cells Right or Shift Cells Down.

4. Click on OK, or press Enter. Excel inserts the cell(s) and shifts the data in the other cells in the specified direction.

FIGURE 12.1   The Insert dialog box.

Drag Insert   A quick way to insert cells is to hold down the Shift key while dragging the fill handle (the little box in the lower right corner of the selected cell(s)). Drag the fill handle up, down, left, or right to set the position of the new cells.

REMOVING CELLS

In Lesson 11, you learned how to clear the contents and formatting of selected cells. This merely removed what was inside the cells. If you want to remove the cells completely, perform the following steps:

1. Select the range of cells you want to delete.

2. Pull down the Edit menu, and choose Delete. The Delete dialog box appears, as shown in Figure 12.2.

3. Select the desired Delete option: Shift Cells Left or Shift Cells Up.

FIGURE 12.2   The Delete dialog box asks where you want surrounding cells shifted.

INSERTING ROWS AND COLUMNS

Inserting entire rows and columns in your worksheet is similar to inserting a cell(s). Here's what you do:

1. Do one of the following:

    *   To insert a single row or column, select a cell. Columns are inserted to the left of the current cell. Rows are inserted above the current cell.

    *   Select the number of columns or rows you want to insert. To select columns, drag over the column letters at the top of the worksheet. To select rows, drag over the row numbers. For example, select three column letters or row numbers to insert three rows or columns.

2. Open the Insert menu.

3. Select Rows or Columns. Excel inserts the row(s) or column(s) and shifts the adjacent rows down or adjacent columns right. Figure 12.3 simulates a worksheet before and after a row is inserted.

Shortcut Insert   To quickly insert rows or columns, select one or more rows or columns, and then right-click on one of them. Choose Insert from the shortcut menu.

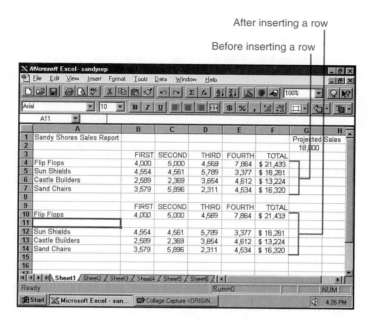

FIGURE 12.3   Inserting a row in a worksheet.

DELETING ROWS AND COLUMNS

Deleting rows and columns is similar to deleting cells. When you delete a row, the rows below the deleted row move up to fill the space. When you delete a column, the columns to the right shift left.

To delete a row or column:

1. Click on the row number or column letter of the row or column you want to delete. You can select more than one row or column by dragging over the row numbers or column letters.

2. Pull down the Edit menu, and choose Delete. Excel deletes the row(s) or column(s) and renumbers the remaining rows and columns sequentially. All cell references in

formulas and names in formulas are updated appropriately, unless they are absolute ($) values (see Lesson 14). Figure 12.4 simulates a worksheet before and after a row is deleted.

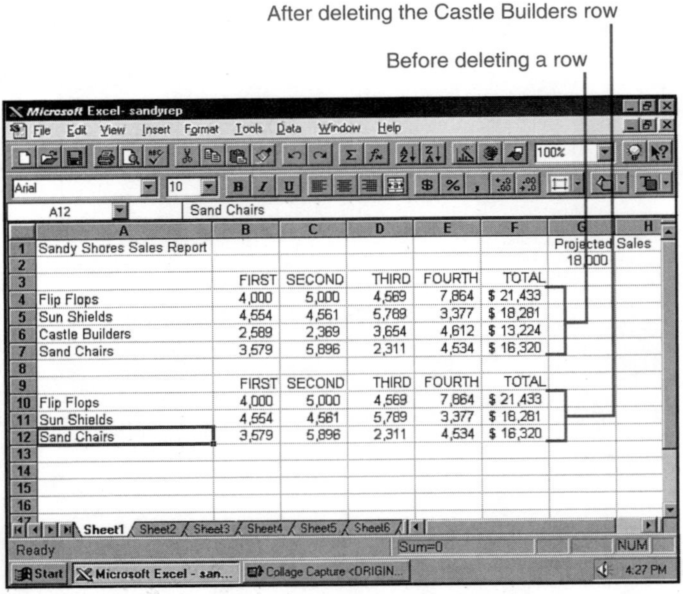

After deleting the Castle Builders row

Before deleting a row

FIGURE 12.4   Deleting a row in a worksheet.

In this lesson, you learned how to insert and delete cells, rows, and columns. In the next lesson, you will learn how to use formulas.

PERFORMING CALCULATIONS WITH FORMULAS

LESSON 13

In this lesson, you will learn how to use formulas to calculate results in your worksheets.

WHAT IS A FORMULA?

Worksheets use formulas to perform calculations on the data you enter. With formulas, you can perform addition, subtraction, multiplication, and division using the values contained in various cells.

Formulas typically consist of one or more cell addresses and/or values and a mathematical operator, such as + (addition), - (subtraction), * (multiplication), or / (division). For example, if you wanted to determine the average of the three values contained in cells A1, B1, and C1, you would type the following formula in the cell where you want the result to appear:

=(A1+B1+C1)/3

 Start Right Every formula must begin with an equal sign (=).

Figure 13.1 shows several formulas in action. Table 13.1 lists the mathematical operators you can use to create formulas.

=E4+E5+E6 gives total
income for the 4th Quarter.

=E7-E14 subtracts expenses
from income to determine profit.

=E10+E11+E12+E13 gives total
expenses for the 4th Quarter.

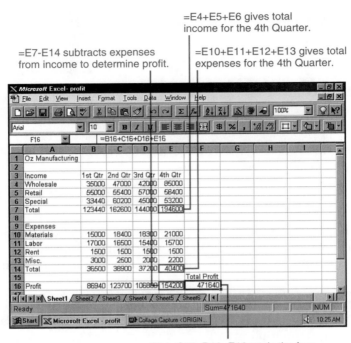

=B16+C16+D16+E16 totals the four
quarter profits to determine total profit.

FIGURE 13.1   Type a formula in the cell where you want the
resulting value to appear.

TABLE 13.1   EXCEL'S MATHEMATICAL OPERATORS.

OPERATOR	PERFORMS	SAMPLE FORMULA	RESULT
^	Exponentiation	=A1^3	Enters the result of raising the value in cell A1 to the third power.
+	Addition	=A1+A2	Enters the total of the values in cells A1 and A2.

OPERATOR	PERFORMS	SAMPLE FORMULA	RESULT
-	Subtraction	=A1-A2	Subtracts the value in cell A2 from the value in cell A1.
*	Multiplication	=A2*3	Multiplies the value in cell A2 by 3.
/	Division	=A1/50	Divides the value in cell A1 by 50.
	Combination	=(A1+A2+A3)/3	Determines the average of the values in cells A1 through A3.

ORDER OF OPERATIONS

Excel performs a series of operations from left to right in the following order, giving some operators precedence over others:

1st   Exponential and equations within parentheses

2nd   Multiplication and division

3rd   Addition and subtraction

This is important to keep in mind when you are creating equations, because the order of operations determines the result.

For example, if you want to determine the average of the values in cells A1, B1, and C1, and you enter =A1+B1+C1/3, you'll probably get the wrong answer. The value in C1 will be divided by 3, and that result will be added to A1+B1. To determine the total of A1 through C1 first, you must enclose that group of values in parentheses: =(A1+B1+C1)/3.

ENTERING FORMULAS

You can enter formulas in either of two ways: by typing the formula or by selecting cell references. To type a formula, perform the following steps:

1. Select the cell in which you want the formula's calculation to appear.

2. Type the equal sign (=).

3. Type the formula. The formula appears in the formula bar.

4. Press Enter, and the result is calculated.

To enter a formula by selecting cell references, take the following steps:

1. Select the cell in which you want the formula's result to appear.

2. Type the equal sign (=).

3. Click on the cell whose address you want to appear first in the formula. The cell address appears in the formula bar.

4. Type a mathematical operator after the value to indicate the next operation you want to perform. The operator appears in the formula bar.

5. Continue clicking on cells and typing operators until the formula is complete.

6. Press Enter to accept the formula or Esc to cancel the operation.

Error!　Make sure that you did not commit one of these common errors: trying to divide by zero or using a blank cell as a divisor in a formula, referring to a blank cell, deleting a cell being used in a formula, or using a range name when you intended to use a single cell address.

DISPLAYING FORMULAS

Excel does not display the actual formula in a cell. Instead, Excel displays the result of the calculation. You can view the formula by selecting the cell and looking in the formula bar. If you want to see the formulas in the cells, do this:

1. Open the Tools menu, and choose Options.

2. Click on the View tab.

3. Click on the Formulas check box in the Window Options area. A check mark appears, indicating that the option has been turned on (see Figure 13.2).

4. Click on OK, or press Enter.

Formulas option

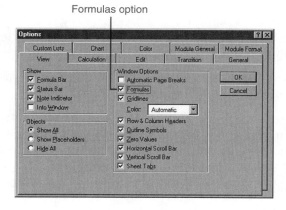

FIGURE 13.2   Using the Options dialog box to display formulas in the cells.

 Display Formulas Quickly   Use the keyboard shortcut, Ctrl+' to toggle between viewing formulas or viewing values. Hold down the Ctrl key, and press ' (the accent key—it's the key with the tilde (~) on it).

EDITING FORMULAS

Editing formulas is the same as editing any other entry in Excel. Here's how you do it:

1. Select the cell that contains the formula you want to edit.

2. Position the insertion point in the formula bar with the mouse, or press F2 to enter Edit mode.

 Quick In-Cell Editing   To quickly edit the contents of a cell, simply double-click on the cell. The insertion point appears inside the cell.

3. Press the up arrow key ↑ or down arrow key ↓ to move the insertion point. Use the Backspace key to delete characters to the left, or the Delete key to delete characters to the right. Type any additional characters.

4. Click on the Enter button on the formula bar, or press Enter to accept your changes.

In this lesson, you learned how to enter and edit formulas. In the next lesson, you will learn how to copy formulas, when to use relative and absolute cell addresses, and how to change Excel's settings for calculating formulas in the worksheet.

COPYING FORMULAS AND RECALCULATION

14

In this lesson, you will learn how to copy formulas, use relative and absolute cell references, and change calculation settings.

COPYING FORMULAS

Copying formulas is similar to copying other data in a worksheet. (For more details, refer to Lesson 11.) To copy formulas:

1. Select the cell that contains the formula you want to copy.

2. Pull down the Edit menu, and select Copy, or press Ctrl+C.

3. Select the cell(s) into which you want to copy the formula. To copy the formula to another worksheet or workbook, change to the new worksheet or workbook.

4. Pull down the Edit menu, and select Paste, or press Ctrl+V.

TIP

Drag and Drop Formulas To quickly copy a formula, use the Drag & Drop feature. Select the cell that contains the formula you want to copy, and then hold down the Ctrl key while dragging the cell selector border where you want the formula copied. When you release the mouse button, the formula is copied to the new location. If you need to copy one formula into two or more cells, use the AutoFill feature as explained in Lesson 4.

Get an Error?   If you get an error after copying a formula, verify the cell references in the copied formula. See the next section, "Using Relative and Absolute Cell Addresses," for more details.

USING RELATIVE AND ABSOLUTE CELL ADDRESSES

When you copy a formula from one place in the worksheet to another, Excel adjusts the cell references in the formulas relative to their new positions in the worksheet. For example, in Figure 14.1, cell B9 contains the formula =B4+B5+B6+B7, which determines the total sales revenue for the first quarter (FIRST). If you copy that formula to cell C9 (to determine the total sales revenue for the second quarter (SECOND), Excel would automatically change the formula to =C4+C5+C6+C7. This is how relative cell addresses work.

Sometimes, you may not want the cell references to be adjusted when formulas are copied. That's when absolute references become important.

Absolute vs. Relative   An *absolute reference* is a cell reference in a formula that does not change when copied to a new location. A *relative reference* is a cell reference in a formula that is adjusted when the formula is copied.

The formula in cells B10, C10, D10, and E10 uses an absolute reference to cell F2, which holds the projected sales for this year. (B10, C10, D10, and E10 divide the sums from row 9 of each column by the contents of cell F2.) If you didn't use an absolute reference, when you copied the formula from B10 to C10, the cell reference would be incorrect, and you would get an error message.

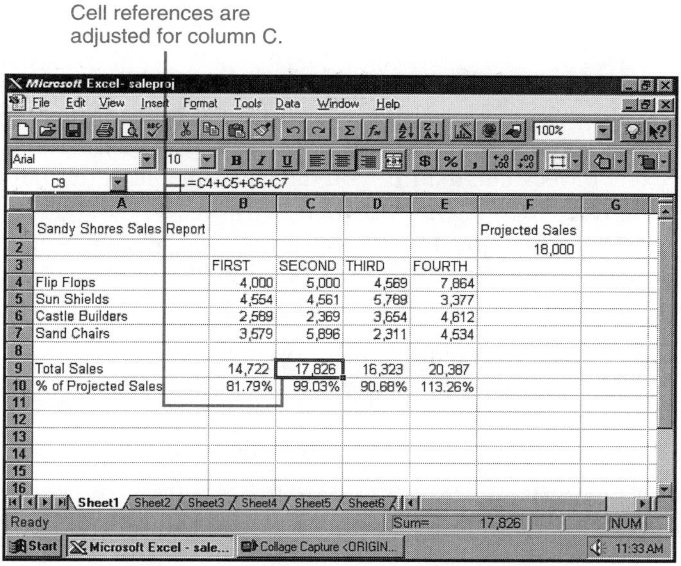

Cell references are
adjusted for column C.

FIGURE 14.1   Excel adjusts cell references when you copy
formulas to different cells.

To make a cell reference in a formula absolute, you must add a $
(dollar sign) before the letter and number that make up the cell
address. For example, the formula in B10 would read as follows:

=B9/F2

You can type the dollar signs yourself or press F4 after typing the
cell address. Some formulas use mixed references. For example,
the column letter may be an absolute reference and the row number may be a relative reference, as in the formula $A2/2. If you
had this formula in cell C2, and you copied it to cell D10, the
result would be the formula $A10/2. The row reference (row num-
ber) would be adjusted, but not the column.

CHANGING THE CALCULATION SETTING

Excel recalculates the formulas in a worksheet every time you edit a value in a cell. However, on a large worksheet, you may not want Excel to recalculate until you have entered all your changes. For example, if you are entering many formulas on a large worksheet, you can speed up the response time by changing from automatic to manual calculation. To change the recalculation setting, take the following steps:

1. Open the Tools menu, and choose Options.

2. Click on the Calculation tab.

3. Select one of the following Calculation options:

    Automatic is the default setting. It recalculates the entire workbook each time you edit or enter a formula.

    Automatic Except Tables automatically recalculates everything except formulas in a data table.

    Manual tells Excel to recalculate only when you say so. To recalculate, you must press F9 or choose the Tools, Options, Calculation command and click the Calc Now button. If you choose Manual, you can turn the Recalculate before Save option off or on.

4. Click the OK button.

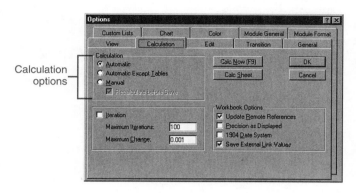

Calculation options

FIGURE 14.2 Change your calculation setting in the Options dialog box.

In this lesson, you learned how to copy formulas. You also learned when to use relative and absolute cell addresses and how to change calculation settings. In the next lesson, you will learn how to use Excel's Function Wizard to insert another type of formula, called a function.

15

PERFORMING CALCULATIONS WITH FUNCTIONS

In this lesson, you will learn how to perform calculations with functions and how to use Excel's new Function Wizard to quickly insert functions in cells.

WHAT ARE FUNCTIONS?

Functions are complex ready-made formulas that perform a series of operations on a specified range of values. For example, to determine the sum of a series of numbers in cells A1 through H1, you can enter the function =SUM(A1:H1), instead of entering =A1+B1+C1+ and so on. Functions can use range references (such as B1:B3), range names (such as SALES), and/or numerical values (such as 585.86).

Every function consists of the following three elements:

- The **=** sign indicates that what follows is a function (formula).

- The **function name** (for example, SUM) indicates the operation that will be performed.

- The **argument** (for example, A1:H1) indicates the cell addresses of the values that the function will act on. The argument is often a range of cells, but it can be much more complex.

You can enter functions either by typing them in cells or by using the Function Wizard, as you'll see later in this lesson.

Table 15.1 shows Excel's most common functions that you'll use in your worksheets.

TABLE 15.1 EXCEL'S MOST COMMON FUNCTIONS

FUNCTION	EXAMPLE	DESCRIPTION
AVERAGE	=AVERAGE(B4:B9)	Calculates the mean or average of a group of numbers.
COUNT	=COUNT(A3:A7)	Counts the numeric values in a range. For example, if a range contains cells with text and other cells with numbers, you can count how many numbers are in that range.
COUNTA	=COUNTA(B4:B10)	Counts all cells that are not blank in a range. For example, if a range contains cells with text and other cells with numbers, you can count how many cells contain text in that range.
IF	=IF(A3>=100,	Uses conditions or "Must be less than tests regarding the 100",A3*2) value of a cell. The condition answer is either true or false. In

continues

Table 15.1   Continued

Function	Example	Description
		the example, if the condition proves true, the first part of the function is calculated (A3<100) and the text `Must be less than 100` is the answer. If the condition proves false, the second part of the function is calculated (A3>100) and A3 is multiplied by 2.
MAX	=MAX(B4:B10)	Returns the maximum value in a range of cells.
MIN	=MIN(B4:B10)	Returns the minimum value in a range of cells.
PMT	=PMT(A3,A4,A5)	Calculates the periodic payment when you enter the interest rate, periods, and principal as arguments.
SUM	=SUM(A1:A10)	Adds the values and calculates the total in a range of cells.

Using the AutoSum Tool

Because SUM is one of the most commonly used functions, Excel created a fast way to enter it—you simply click on the AutoSum button in the Standard toolbar. AutoSum guesses what cells you want summed, based on the currently selected cell. If AutoSum selects an incorrect range of cells, you can edit the selection.

To use AutoSum

1. Select the cell in which you want the sum inserted. Try to choose a cell at the end of a row or column of data.

2. Click on the AutoSum tool in the Standard toolbar. AutoSum inserts =SUM and the range of the cells to the left of or above the selected cell (see Figure 15.1).

3. You can adjust the range of cells by doing one of the following

   - Click inside the selected cell or the formula bar, and edit the range.

   - Click on the first correct cell in the range to deselect the incorrect range, then drag the mouse pointer over the rest of the correct range of cells.

4. Click on the Enter box in the formula bar, or press Enter. The total for the selected range is calculated.

 TIP   **Quickie AutoSum**   To quickly insert the sum function, select the cell in which you want the sum inserted and double-click on the AutoSum tool on the Standard toolbar. By double-clicking instead of single-clicking on the AutoSum tool, you bypass displaying the SUM formula and its arguments in the cell. Instead, you see the total in the cell and the SUM formula in the formula bar.

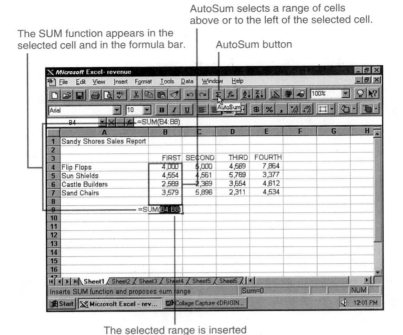

AutoSum selects a range of cells above or to the left of the selected cell.

The SUM function appears in the selected cell and in the formula bar.

AutoSum button

The selected range is inserted as the function's argument.

FIGURE 15.1   AutoSum inserts the SUM function and selects the cells it plans to total.

USING THE AUTOCALCULATE

When you wanted to quickly check a total in earlier versions of Excel, did you ever use a calculator or enter temporary formulas on a worksheet? If you did, you might find Excel's new AutoCalculate feature very handy. AutoCalculate lets you quickly check a total or an average, count entries or numbers, and find the maximum or minumum number in a range.

Here's how AutoCalculate works:

- To check a total, select the range you want to sum. Excel will automatically display the answer in the Auto-Calculate area (on the right side of the status bar at the bottom of the screen).

- If you want to perform a different function on a range of numbers, select the range and click the right mouse button on the AutoCalculate area to display the shortcut menu. Then choose a function from the menu. For example, choose Count to count the numeric values in the range. The answer will display in the AutoCalculate area.

USING FUNCTION WIZARD

Although you can type a function directly into a cell, just as you can type formulas, you may find it easier to use the Function Wizard. The Function Wizard leads you through the process of inserting a function. Here's how you do it:

1. Select the cell in which you want to insert the function. (You can insert a function by itself or as part of a formula.)

2. Open the Insert menu, and choose Function, or click on the Function Wizard button (the fx button) on the Standard toolbar or formula bar. The Function Wizard-Step 1 of 2 dialog box appears, as shown in Figure 15.2.

 Function Names   If this is your first encounter with functions, don't expect them to be simple. However, you can learn a lot about a function and what it does by reading the descriptions in the dialog box. Whenever you highlight a function name, Excel displays a description of the function. If you need more help, click on the Help button, or press F1.

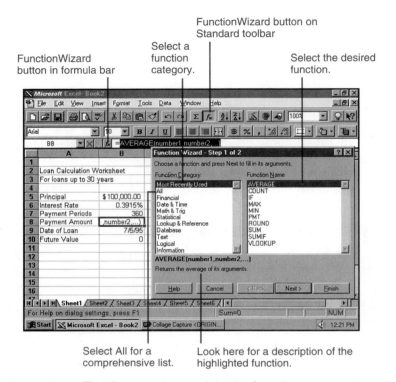

FunctionWizard button on Standard toolbar

FunctionWizard button in formula bar

Select a function category.

Select the desired function.

Select All for a comprehensive list.

Look here for a description of the highlighted function.

FIGURE 15.2 The first step is to select the function you want to use.

3. In the Function Category list, select the type of function you want to insert. Excel displays the names of the available functions in the Function Name list.

4. Select the function you want to insert from the Function Name list, and then click on the Next button. Excel displays the Step 2 of 2 dialog box. This box will differ depending on the selected function. Figure 15.3 shows the dialog box you'll see if you chose the PMT function.

5. Enter the values or cell ranges for the argument. You can type a value or argument, or drag the dialog box title bar out of the way and click on the desired cells with the mouse pointer.

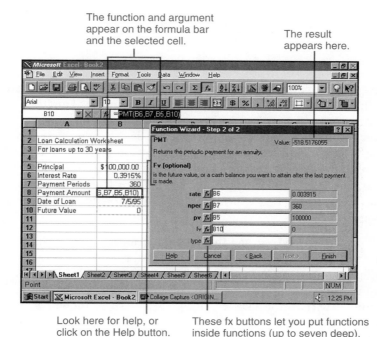

The function and argument appear on the formula bar and the selected cell.

The result appears here.

Look here for help, or click on the Help button.

These fx buttons let you put functions inside functions (up to seven deep).

FIGURE 15.3   The second step is to enter the values and cell references that make up the argument.

6. Click on the Finish button. Excel inserts the function and argument in the selected cell and displays the result. The result appears in red, which indicates a negative number. This negative number represents the amount you must pay for the loan.

Low Interest Rates   If the interest rate shown in Figure 15.3 looks too good to be true, it's because Excel works with monthly percentage rates rather than annual percentage rates. Whenever you enter a percent on a loan or investment, enter the annual percentage rate divided by 12. For example, if your mortgage is at 7% (.07), you would enter =.07/12.

To edit a function, you can type your corrections just as you can with a formula (see Lesson 13). You can also use the Function Wizard. To use the Wizard, select the cell that contains the function you want to edit. (You want the cell selected, but you don't want to be in Edit mode; that is, the insertion point should not be displayed in the cell.) Open the Insert menu, and choose Function, or click on the Function Wizard button. The Editing Function 1 of 1 dialog box appears, allowing you to edit the function's argument.

In this lesson, you learned the basics of dealing with functions, and you learned how to use Excel's Function Wizard to quickly enter functions. You also learned how to quickly total a series of numbers with the AutoSum tool and how to check the sum of numbers with AutoCalculate. In the next lesson, you will learn how to improve the look of your text by adding character and number formatting and alignment.

ADJUSTING NUMBER FORMATS AND TEXT ALIGNMENT

In this lesson, you will learn how to customize the appearance of numbers in your worksheet and control the alignment of text inside cells.

FORMATTING VALUES

Numeric values are usually more than just numbers. They represent a dollar value, a date, a percent, or some other value. You can select the format type that appears as a real value in the Format Cells dialog box or you can customize a format to display the value in a certain format. Excel offers a wide range of number formats, as listed in Table 16.1.

TABLE 16.1 EXCEL'S NUMBER FORMATS

NUMBER FORMAT	EXAMPLE	DESCRIPTION
General	$3,400.50	Default number format. Has no specific number format. With General format, you can type a number with a decimal point, dollar sign, comma, or percent sign, a date, time, or fraction in a cell. Excel will automatically display the value with the format you entered.

continues

TABLE 16.1 CONTINUED

NUMBER FORMAT	EXAMPLE	DESCRIPTION
Number	3,400.50	Use for general display of numbers. The default Number format is two decimal places, a comma for a thousand separator, and negative numbers are black preceded by a minus sign. You can display the number of decimal places, whether or not you want a comma for a thousand separator, and negative numbers in red or black, preceded by a minus sign or enclosed in parentheses.
Currency	$3,400.50	Use for general monetary values. The default Currency format is two decimal places, a dollar sign, and negative numbers are black preceded by a minus sign. You can display the number of decimal places, whether or not you want a dollar sign, and negative numbers in red or black, preceded by a minus sign or enclosed in parentheses.
Accounting	$3,400.00	Use for aligning dollar signs and decimal points in a column. The default Accounting format is two

NUMBER FORMAT	EXAMPLE	DESCRIPTION
		decimal places and a dollar sign. You can specify the number of decimal places and whether or not you want a dollar sign.
Date	8/7	Use to display date and time serial numbers as date values with slashes or hyphens. The default Date format is the month and day separated by a slash. To display only the time portion, use Time format.
Time	10:00	The default Time format is the hour and minutes separated by a colon. Use to display date and time serial numbers as time values with hours, minutes, seconds, AM or PM. Then you can perform calculations on the time values. To display only the date portion, use Date format.
Percentage	99.50%	The default Percentage format is two decimal places. Multiplies the value in a cell by 100 and displays the result with a percent sign.

continues

TABLE 16.1   CONTINUED

NUMBER FORMAT	EXAMPLE	DESCRIPTION
Fraction	1/2	The default Fraction format is up to one digit on either side of the slash. Use to display the number of digits you want on either side of the slash and the fraction type such as halves, quarters, eighths, and so on.
Scientific	3.40E+03	The default Scientific format is two decimal places. Use to display numbers in scientfic notation.
Text	135RV90	Use to display both text and numbers in a cell as text. Excel displays the entry exactly as typed.
Special	02110	Use to display ZIP code, phone number, and Social Security numbers in a list or database.
Custom	00.0%	Use to create your own number format. You can use any of the format codes in the Type list and then make changes to those codes. # represents a number placeholder, and 0 represents a zero placeholder.

After deciding on a suitable numeric format, follow these steps:

1. Select the cell or range that contains the values you want to format.

2. Pull down the Format menu, and select Cells, or press Ctrl+1. The Format Cells dialog box appears.

3. If the Number tab is not up front, click on it. (See Figure 16.1.)

4. In the Category list, select the numeric format category you want to use. The sample box displays the formats in that category in the Type list.

5. In the Type list, select the format type you want to use. When you select a format type, Excel shows you what a sample number would look like formatted with that type.

6. Click OK, or press Enter.

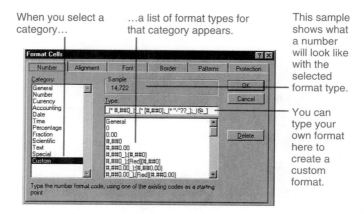

FIGURE 16.1   The Format Cells dialog box with the Number tab up front.

The Formatting toolbar (just below the Standard toolbar) contains several buttons for selecting a number format, including the following:

   Currency Style

   Percent Style

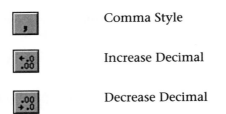

Comma Style

Increase Decimal

Decrease Decimal

Select the cell and then click on a formatting tool. You can also change the Number format of a cell by using the shortcut menu; select the cell, click the right mouse button on the cell to display the shortcut menu, and then choose Format Cells.

Formatting Dates and Times

Dates and time are actually numeric values that have been formatted to appear as dates and times. You can change the way Excel displays the date and time if you like. Excel offers several date and time formats as listed in Table 16.2.

Table 16.2   Excel's date and time formats

Date/Time Format	Example
m/d	4/8
m/d/yy	4/8/95
mm/dd/yy	04/08/95
d-mmm	8-Apr
d-mmm-y	8-Apr-95
dd-mmm-y	08-Apr-95
mmm-yy	Apr-95
mmmm-yy	April-95

DATE/TIME FORMAT	EXAMPLE
mmmm-d, yyyy	April 8, 1995
m/d/yy h:mm	4/8/95 5:30
m/d/yy hh:mm	4/8/95 17:30
hh:mm	17:15
h:mm	5:15
h:mm:ss	5:15:20
mm:ss	20:45
h:mm AM/PM	5:15 PM
h:mm:ss AM/PM	5:15:20 AM

After deciding on a suitable date and time format, follow these steps:

1. Select the cell or range that contains the dates or times you want to format.

2. Pull down the Format menu, and select Cells, or press Ctrl+1. The Format Cells dialog box appears.

3. If the Number tab is not up front, click on it.

4. In the Category list, select the date or time format category. Excel displays the formats in that category in the Type list. (See Figure 16.2.)

5. In the Type list, select the format type you want to use. When you select a format type, Excel shows you what a sample date or time would look like formatted with that type.

6. Click OK, or press Enter.

This sample shows what a date will look
like with the selected format type.

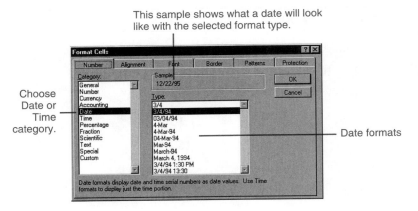

Choose
Date or
Time
category.

Date formats

FIGURE 16.2   The date formats.

ALIGNING TEXT IN CELLS

When you enter data into an Excel worksheet, that data is aligned
automatically. Text is aligned on the left, and numbers are
aligned on the right. Text and numbers are initially set at the
bottom of the cells.

To change the alignment:

1. Select the cell or range you want to align.

   If you want to center a title or other text over a range of
   cells, select the entire range of blank cells in which you
   want the text centered, including the cell that contains
   the text you want to center.

2. Pull down the Format menu, and select Cells, or press
   Ctrl+1. The Format Cells dialog box appears.

3. Click the Alignment tab. The alignment options jump up
   front as shown in Figure 16.3.

4. Choose from the following options and option groups to set the alignment:

Horizontal lets you specify a left/right alignment in the cell(s). (The Center across selection option lets you center a title or other text inside a range of cells.)

Vertical lets you specify how you want the text aligned in relation to the top and bottom of the cell(s).

Orientation lets you flip the text sideways or print it from top to bottom (rather than left to right).

Wrap Text tells Excel to wrap long lines of text within a cell without changing the width of cell. (Normally, Excel displays all text in a cell on one line.)

5. Click OK, or press Enter.

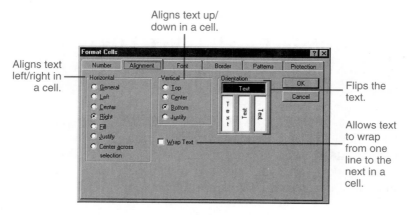

FIGURE 16.3   The Alignment options.

Repeat Performance   To repeat the alignment format command in another cell, use the Repeat Format Cells command from the Edit menu, or click the Repeat button in the Standard toolbar.

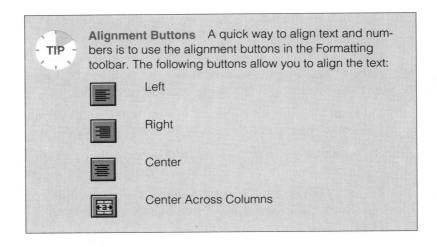

Alignment Buttons   A quick way to align text and numbers is to use the alignment buttons in the Formatting toolbar. The following buttons allow you to align the text:

Left

Right

Center

Center Across Columns

Changing the Default Format and Alignment

When you enter the same type of data into a large worksheet, it is sometimes convenient to change the default format. You then can change the format for only those cells that are exceptions. Note that when you change the default, it affects all the cells in the worksheet and every sheet in the workbook. When you create a new workbook, Excel uses the default format settings, not the modified version of the format settings.

You can change the default settings for number format, alignment, and others. To change the defaults:

1. Open the Format menu, and choose Style. The Style dialog box appears.

2. In the Style Name list box, select Normal.

3. Click the Modify button. Excel displays the Format Cells dialog box, as shown in Figure 16.1.

4. Click the tab for the group of format settings you want to change. For example, you can click Number to change the default numeric formatting.

5. Select the desired format settings, such as Currency with 0 decimal places, and then click the OK button. Excel returns you to the Style dialog box.

6. Click OK, or press Enter.

In this lesson, you learned how to format numbers and align data in cells. In the next lesson, you will learn how to format text.

GIVING YOUR TEXT A NEW LOOK

In this lesson, you will learn how to change the appearance of the text in the cells.

HOW YOU CAN MAKE TEXT LOOK DIFFERENT

When you type text or numbers, Excel inserts it in the Arial font, which doesn't look very fancy. You can change the following text attributes to improve the appearance of your text or set it apart from other text:

Font For example, Algerian, Desdemona, and Wide Latin.

Font Style For example, Bold, Italic, Underline, and Strikethrough.

Size For example, 10-point, 12-point, and 20-point. (The higher the point size, the bigger the text is. There are approximately 72 points in an inch.)

Color For example, Red, Magenta, and Cyan.

What's a Font? In Excel, a font is a set of characters that have the same typeface. A typeface is all type of a single design, for example, Helvetica. When you select a font, Excel also allows you to change the font's size, add an optional *attribute* to the font, such as bold or italic; underline the text; change its color; or add special effects such as strikethrough, superscript, subscript, and small caps.

Figure 17.1 shows a worksheet after different attributes have been changed for selected text.

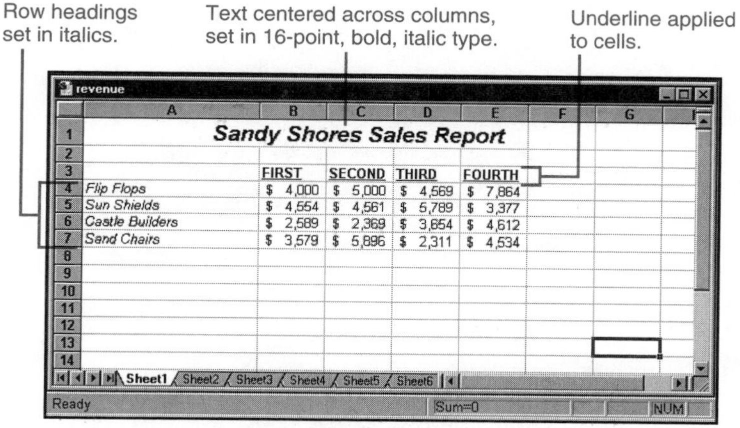

Row headings set in italics.

Text centered across columns, set in 16-point, bold, italic type.

Underline applied to cells.

FIGURE 17.1 A sampling of several text attributes.

USING THE FORMAT CELLS DIALOG BOX

You can change the look of your text by using the Format Cells dialog box or by using the Font buttons in the Formatting toolbar. To use the Format Cells dialog box, follow these steps:

1. Select the cell or range that contains the text you want to format.

2. Open the Format menu, and choose Cells, or press Ctrl+1. (You can also right-click on the selected cells, and choose Format Cells from the shortcut menu.)

3. Click the Font tab. The Font options jump to the front, as shown in Figure 17.2.

4. Enter your font preferences by selecting them from the lists.

5. Click OK, or press Enter.

Excel uses a default font to style your text as you type it. To change the default font, enter your font preferences in the Font tab, and then click on the Normal Font option. When you click the OK button, Excel makes your preferences the default font.

Check the Preview area to see
the effects of your choices.

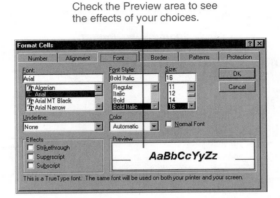

FIGURE 17.2   The Format Cells dialog box with the Font tab up front.

Font Shortcuts   A faster way to change text attributes is to use the keyboard shortcuts. First select the cell(s), then press Ctrl+B for bold; Ctrl+I for Italic; Ctrl+U for Underline; and Ctrl+5 for Strikethrough.

CHANGING TEXT ATTRIBUTES WITH TOOLBAR BUTTONS

A faster way to enter font changes is to use the buttons and drop-down lists in the Formatting toolbar, as shown in Figure 17.3.

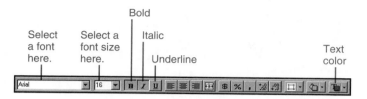

FIGURE 17.3 Use the Formatting toolbar to quickly make font changes.

To use a tool to change text attributes:

1. Select the cell or range that contains the text whose look you want to change.

2. To change the font or font size, pull down the appropriate drop-down list, and click on the font or size you want. You can also type the point size in the Font Size box.

3. To add an attribute (such as bold or underlining), click on the desired button.

TIP   **Change Before You Type**   You can activate the attributes you want before you type text. For example, if you want a title in Bold, 12-point MS Sans Serif, click in the document to position the insertion point where you want to change the attributes, then set these attributes before you start typing.

In this lesson, you learned how to customize your text to achieve the look you want. In the next lesson, you will learn how to add borders and shading to your worksheet.

LESSON 18

ADDING CELL BORDERS AND SHADING

In this lesson, you will learn how to add pizzazz to your worksheets by adding borders and shading.

As you work with your worksheet on-screen, each cell is identified by a gridline that surrounds the cell. In print, these gridlines may appear washed out. To have better defined lines appear on the printout, you can add borders to selected cells or cell ranges. Figure 18.1 shows the options for adding lines around cells and cell ranges.

All	All		Outline	Outline		Dotted line	Dotted line
All	All		Outline	Outline		Dotted line	Dotted line
All	All		Outline	Outline		Dotted line	Dotted line
Single	Single		Double	Double		Thick	Thick
Single	Single		Double	Double		Thick	Thick
Single	Single		Double	Double		Thick	Thick
Top	Top		Bottom	Bottom		Left	Right
Top	Top		Bottom	Bottom		Left	Right
Top	Top		Bottom	Bottom		Left	Right

FIGURE 18.1 A sampling of borders.

TIP

Hiding Gridlines   When adding borders to a worksheet, hide the gridlines to get a better idea of how the borders will print. Open the Tools menu, select Options, click on the View tab, and select Gridlines to remove the check mark from the check box. By default, Excel for Windows 95 does not print the gridlines. In previous versions of Excel, the gridlines print by default; however, you can turn off the default to prevent the gridlines from printing.

To add borders to a cell or range, perform the following steps:

1. Select the cell(s) around which you want a border to appear.

2. Open the Format menu, and choose Cells. The Format Cells dialog box appears.

3. Click the Border tab. The Border options jump up front, as shown in Figure 18.2.

4. Select the desired border position, style (thickness), and color for the border.

5. Click OK, or press Enter.

Select a border position.   Select a border style.

Select a border color.

FIGURE 18.2   The Format Cells dialog box with the Border tab up front.

TIP

Borders Button   To add borders quickly, select the cells around which you want the border to appear, and then click on the arrow to the right of the Borders button in the Formatting toolbar. Click on the desired border. If you click on the Borders button itself (rather than on the arrow), Excel automatically adds a bottom borderline or the borderline you last chose to the selected cells.

ADDING SHADING TO CELLS

For a simple but dramatic effect, add shading to your worksheets. Figure 18.3 illustrates the effects that you can create with shading.

To add shading to a cell or range:

1. Select the cell(s) you want to shade.

2. Pull down the Format menu, and choose Cells.

3. Click on the Patterns tab. The shading options jump to the front, as shown in Figure 18.4.

4. Click the down arrow next to Pattern, and you will see a grid that contains all the colors from the color palette, as well as patterns. Select the shading color and pattern you want to use. The Color options let you choose a color for the overall shading. The Pattern options let you select a black-and-white or colored pattern that lies on top of the overall shading. A preview of the result is displayed in the Sample box.

5. Click OK, or press Enter.

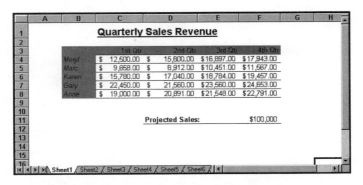

FIGURE 18.3   A worksheet with added shading.

Select an overall color   Select a pattern to lay
for the selected cell.   on top of the color.

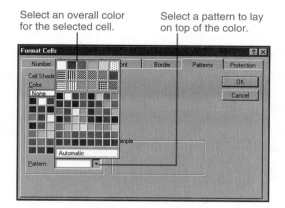

FIGURE 18.4   Selecting a shading and a pattern.

 Color Button   A quick way to add cell shading (without
a pattern) is to select the cells you want to shade and
then click on the arrow to the right of the Color button (the
button that has the bucket on it). Click on the color you
want to use. If the shading is dark, consider using the
Font Color button (just to the right of the Color button) to
select a light color for the text.

USING AUTOFORMAT

Excel offers the AutoFormat feature that takes some of the pain
out of formatting. AutoFormat provides you with 16 predesigned
table formats that you can apply to a worksheet.

To use predesigned formats, perform the following steps:

1. Select the worksheet(s) and cell(s) that contain the data
   you want to format.

2. Open the Format menu, and choose AutoFormat. The
   AutoFormat dialog box appears, as shown in Figure 18.5.

3. In the Table Format list, choose the predesigned format you want to use. When you select a format, Excel shows you what it will look like in the Sample area.

4. To exclude certain elements from the AutoFormat, click on the Options button, and choose the formats you want to turn off.

5. Click the OK button. Excel formats your table to make it look like the one in the preview area.

Select a predesigned table format.

Sample area shows effects of the table format.

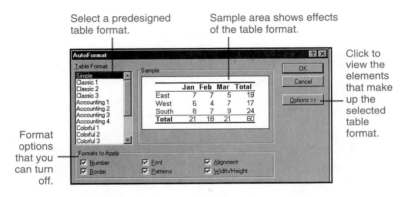

Click to view the elements that make up the selected table format.

Format options that you can turn off.

FIGURE 18.5   Use the AutoFormat dialog box to select a prefab format.

Deformatting an AutoFormat   If you don't like what AutoFormat did to your worksheet, select the table, open the Format menu, and choose AutoFormat. From the Table Format list, choose None to remove the AutoFormat.

COPYING FORMATS WITH FORMAT PAINTER

Excel gives you two ways to copy and paste formatting:

- You can use the Edit Copy command and then the Edit Paste Special command and select Formats from the Paste options in the Paste Special dialog box.

- You can use the Format Painter button in the Standard toolbar.

The Format Painter lets you quickly copy and paste formats that you have already used in a workbook. Because the Format Painter button is faster, I'll give you the steps you need to paint formats:

1. Select the cell(s) that contain the formatting you want to copy and paste.

2. Click on the Format Painter button (the one with the paintbrush on it) in the Standard toolbar. Excel copies the formatting. The mouse pointer changes into a paintbrush with a plus sign next to it.

3. Click and drag over the cells to which you want to apply the copied formatting.

4. Release the mouse button. The copied formatting is applied to the selected cells.

In this lesson, you learned some additional ways to enhance the appearance of your worksheets. In the next lesson, you will learn how to change the sizes of rows and columns.

CHANGING COLUMN WIDTH AND ROW HEIGHT

In this lesson, you will learn how to adjust the column width and row height to make the best use of the worksheet space. You can set these manually or let Excel make the adjustments for you with its AutoFit feature.

ADJUSTING COLUMN WIDTH AND ROW HEIGHT WITH A MOUSE

You can adjust the width of a column or the height of a row by using a dialog box or by dragging with the mouse. Here's how you adjust the row height or column width with the mouse:

1. To change the row height or column width for one row or column, skip to Step 2. For two or more rows or columns, click and drag over the headings for the rows or columns with the mouse pointer. Then release the mouse button.

2. Move the mouse pointer to one of the row heading or column heading borders, as shown in Figure 19.1. (Use the right border of the column heading to adjust column width or the bottom border of the row heading to adjust the row height.)

3. Hold down the mouse button and drag the border.

4. Release the mouse button, and the row height or column width is adjusted.

Dragging the right border of
column C changes its width.

	A	B	C	D	E	F	G	H
1			Quarterly Sales Revenue					
2								
3			1st Qtr.	2nd Qtr.	3rd Qtr.	4th Qtr.		
4		Meryl	$ 12,500.00	$ 15,800.00	$16,897.00	$17,943.00		
5		Marc	$ 9,658.00	$ 8,912.00	$10,451.00	$11,567.00		
6		Karen	$ 15,780.00	$ 17,040.00	$18,764.00	$19,457.00		
7		Gary	$ 22,450.00	$ 21,560.00	$23,580.00	$24,653.00		
8		Anne	$ 19,000.00	$ 20,891.00	$21,548.00	$22,791.00		
9								
10								
11			Projected Sales:		$100,000			
12								
13								
14								
15								
16								

Sheet1 / Sheet2 / Sheet3 / Sheet4 / Sheet5 / Sheet6 /

FIGURE 19.1   The mouse pointer changes to a double-headed arrow when you move it over a border in the row or column heading.

Dragging the border of a row or column does not give as precise sizing as when you provide specific sizes with the Format Row Height and Format Column Width commands.

TIP

Custom-Fit Cells   To quickly make a column as wide as its widest entry, double-click on the right border of the column heading. To make a row as tall as its tallest entry, double-click on the bottom border of the row heading. To change more than one column or row at a time, click and drag over the desired row or column headings and then double-click on the bottommost or rightmost heading border.

USING THE FORMAT MENU

The Format menu contains the commands you need to change the column width and row height of selected rows and columns. Here's how you use the Format menu to change the column width:

1. Select the column(s) whose width you want to change. To change the width of a single column, select any cell in that column.

2. Pull down the Format menu, select Column, and select Width. The Column Width dialog box appears, as shown in Figure 19.2.

3. Type the number of characters you would like as the width. The default width is 8.43.

4. Click OK, or press Enter.

FIGURE 19.2   Changing the column width.

 TIP   **AutoFit Column Width**   To make columns as wide as their widest entries, select the columns, open the Format menu, select Column, and select AutoFit Selection.

By default, Excel makes a row a bit taller than the tallest text in the row. For example, if the tallest text is 10 points tall, Excel makes the row 12.75 points tall. To use the Format menu to change the row height:

1. Select the row(s) whose height you want to change. To change the height of a single row, select any cell in that row.

2. Pull down the Format menu, select Row and then Height. The Row Height dialog box appears, as shown in Figure 19.3.

3. Type the desired height in points.

4. Click OK, or press Enter.

FIGURE 19.3   Changing the row height.

In this lesson, you learned how to change the row height and column width. In the next lesson, you will learn how to use styles (collections of text format settings).

FORMATTING WITH STYLES

In this lesson, you'll learn how to apply several formatting effects by applying a single style to selected cells.

WHAT IS A STYLE?

In Lessons 16 through 18, you enhanced a spreadsheet by applying various formats to cells. Styles allow you to apply several formats to a selected cell or cell block with just one step by assigning a named style.

What's a Style? A style is a group of cell formatting options that you can apply to a cell or cell block. If you change the style's definition later, that change affects the formatting of all cells formatted with that style.

Each style contains specifications for one or more of the following options:

- **Number** Controls the appearance of values, such as dollar values and dates.

- **Font** Specifies the type style, type size, and any attributes for text contained in the cell (such as bold, italic, or underline).

- **Alignment** Specifies general, left, right, or center alignment.

- **Border** Specifies the border placement and line style options for the cell.

- **Patterns**   Adds specified shading to the cell.

- **Protection**   Allows you to protect or unprotect a cell. By protecting cells in your worksheet, you lock the cells so that they cannot be edited or deleted. However, if you protect a cell or range of cells, the cells are not locked until you protect a worksheet as well by selecting Tools, Protection, Protect Sheet.

Excel has six precreated styles:

Normal   The default style. Number is set to General (lets you enter a value with a decimal point, dollar sign, comma, or percent sign, and as a date or time), Font to Arial, Size to 10-point, Alignment of numbers is right, and Alignment of text is left, No Border, No Pattern, and Protection is set to locked.

Comma   Number is set to the Comma style with 2 decimal places. Negative numbers are black and enclosed in parentheses.

Comma (0)   Number is set to the Comma style with 0 decimal places. Negative numbers are black and enclosed in parentheses.

Currency   Number is set to the Currency style with 2 decimal places. Negative numbers are black and enclosed in parentheses.

Currency (0)   Number is set to the Currency style with 0 decimal places. Negative numbers are black and enclosed in parentheses.

Percent   Number is set to the Percent style with 0 decimal places. Negative numbers are black and are preceded by a minus sign.

Style Buttons You can apply most of Excel's existing styles by selecting the cell or cell range and then clicking on the appropriate button in the Formatting toolbar. For example, to set the currency format, select the cells, and then click on the Currency Style button (the button with the dollar sign on it).

APPLYING EXISTING STYLES

To apply an existing style to a cell or range, perform the following steps:

1. Select the cell or range.

2. Open the Format menu, and select Style. The Style dialog box appears, as shown in Figure 20.1.

3. Click the down arrow to the right of the Style Name list box, and select the style you want to use.

4. Click OK or press Enter. The style is applied to the selected cell or range. Anything you type in this cell or range will be formatted according to the style you selected.

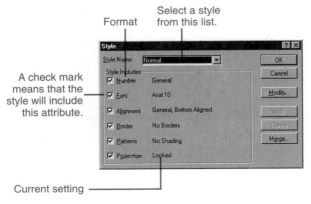

FIGURE 20.1 Use the Style dialog box to apply styles to cells.

CREATING STYLES

To save time, save your favorite formatting combinations as styles. You can create your own styles in various ways:

- Define the style: Create a style, and then assign one or more formatting attributes to it.

- Define by example: Select a cell that contains the formatting you want to use, and then create a style based on that cell.

- Copy a format: Select a cell in another workbook that contains the formatting you want to use, and then copy it to the list of styles used in the current workbook.

DEFINING A STYLE

To define a style, perform the following steps:

1. Open the Format menu, and choose Style. The Style dialog box appears.

2. Type a name for the style in the Style Name list box, and click on the Add button. The style is added to the list, and you can now modify it.

3. Remove the check mark from any check box whose attribute you do not want to include in the style. (See Figure 20.2.)

4. To change any of the format settings for the attributes in the list, click on the Modify button. Excel displays the Format Cells dialog box. (See Figure 20.3.)

5. Click on the tab for the format attribute whose settings you want to change, and enter your preferences.

6. Repeat step 5 for each attribute whose settings you want to change.

7. Click OK, or press Enter. You return to the Style dialog box.

8. Click OK, or press Enter. The style is created and saved.

Type a name for
the new style.

Turn a
format
attribute on
or off.

Click on Modify
to change the
format settings.

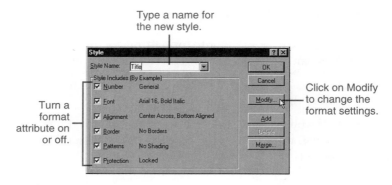

FIGURE 20.2   Defining a new style.

Click on a tab for the format
attribute you want to change.

Change
any of the
format
settings.

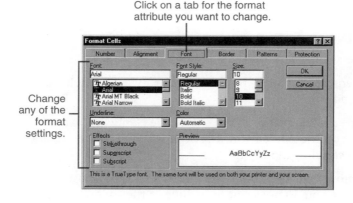

FIGURE 20.3   Modifying a style in the Format Cells dialog box.

CREATING A NEW STYLE BY EXAMPLE

To create a new style by example:

1. Select a cell whose formatting you want to use.

2. Open the Format menu, and choose Style.

3. Type a name for the style in the Style Name box.

4. Click the Add button. The named style with the formatting from the selected cell is added to the Style Name list box.

5. Click OK, or press Enter.

COPYING EXISTING STYLES

To copy existing styles from another workbook:

1. Open both workbooks.

2. Switch to the workbook you want to copy the styles to.

3. Open the Format menu, and choose Style.

4. Click the Merge button.

5. Select the name of the worksheet to copy from.

6. Click OK, or press Enter to close the Merge dialog box. If the dialog box asks, "Merge styles that have the same names?" click Yes.

7. Click OK, or press Enter. All the existing styles from the workbook are copied to the current workbook.

In this lesson, you learned how to create and apply styles. In the next lesson, you will learn how to work with templates.

LESSON 21

WORKING WITH TEMPLATES

In this lesson, you'll learn how to create a workbook with an Excel template and customize templates.

WHAT IS A TEMPLATE?

Every workbook is based on a template. The default template is NORMAL.XLT. A template can help you create workbooks that are consistent and customize your workbooks to suit a particular need. For example, if you create a weekly budget report and don't want to re-create the entire report each week, you can just save one of your reports (or use one of Excel's built-in templates) as a template, and then insert new numbers in the basic format each week.

When you save the workbook as a template or use an Excel built-in template, you can create additional workbooks based on the template. These workbooks will include the same text, formatting, and other elements you included when you created the template.

What's a Template? A template is a collection of patterns and tools for creating a category of workbooks. You can format the template, insert text and graphics, and change the page layout so that the template includes all the key information.

CREATING A WORKBOOK WITH AN EXCEL TEMPLATE

To create a workbook with an Excel template, perform the following steps:

1. Open the File menu, and select New. The New dialog box appears, showing two tabs: General and Spreadsheet Solutions.

2. Click on the Spreadsheet Solutions tab, and click on the template icon you want to use. You see a sample of the template in the Preview area, as shown in Figure 21.1.

3. Click OK or press Enter. Excel copies the template into a new workbook, ready for you to add your own information to it.

Click on the template icon you want. Click the Spreadsheet Solutions tab to see the available built-in templates. Selected template shows in the Preview area.

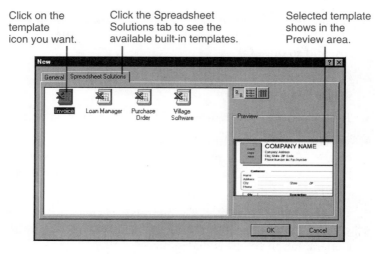

FIGURE 21.1   Use the New dialog box to create a new workbook based on a built-in template.

Built-In Templates   Excel for Windows 95 provides various built-in templates that can help you plan your finances and run your business. Some of these templates include Invoice, Loan Manager, Purchase Order, Village Software, and much more. The Village Software template allows you to order customized spreadsheets from a "software company." The Spreadsheet Solutions tab and built-in templates are new in Excel 95. In Excel 5, you could only create a template from an existing workbook.

CREATING A TEMPLATE

To save time, save your favorite workbook as a template. You can create your template based on an existing workbook.

To create a template, perform the following steps:

1. Create the workbook or open the workbook you want to save as a template. You can include text, formatting, macros, and so on.

2. Open the File menu, and choose Save As. The Save As dialog box appears.

3. Type a name for the template in the File Name text box.

4. Select Template from the Save as Type drop-down list box. You'll see the Templates folder appear in the Save In box. All templates must be stored in the Templates folder. (See Figure 21.2.)

5. Click Save, or press Enter. The template is created and saved. When you use this template, you will find it on the General tab in the New dialog box.

Save all your templates in the Templates folder.

Type a name for the new template here.

Select Template in the Save as Type drop-down list box.

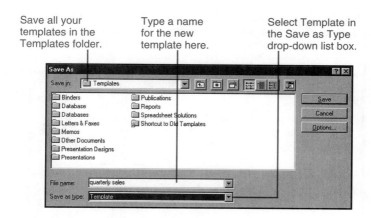

FIGURE 21.2 Creating a new template.

CUSTOMIZING A TEMPLATE

You can modify a built-in template at any time. For instance, you can add a note to a cell in the template, hide the CellTips in the template, or add your company information to the template.

To customize a template, you can do the following:

1. Open the workbook that contains the template you want to customize, as shown in Figure 21.3.

2. Click the Customize button at the top of the template. Excel inserts a new worksheet before the template worksheet. For example, the Customize Your Invoice worksheet appears before the Invoice worksheet.

3. Make the changes to the customized template.

TIP

CellTips You can use Excel for Windows 95's new CellTips feature to enter information in the template. CellTips are the same as cell notes. For more information on CellTips, see Lesson 5.

Use the Template toolbar to select template options.

Move the mouse pointer over a CellTip (red dot) to display helpful information.

Click Customize to customize your template.

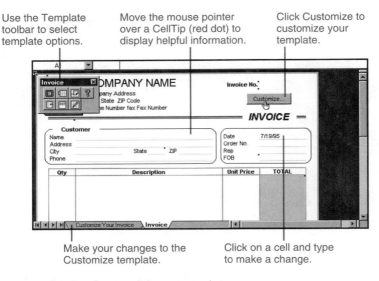

Make your changes to the Customize template.

Click on a cell and type to make a change.

FIGURE 21.3   Customizing a template.

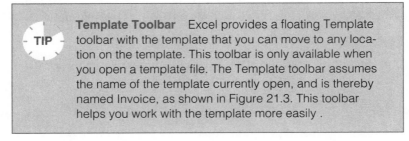

Template Toolbar   Excel provides a floating Template toolbar with the template that you can move to any location on the template. This toolbar is only available when you open a template file. The Template toolbar assumes the name of the template currently open, and is thereby named Invoice, as shown in Figure 21.3. This toolbar helps you work with the template more easily .

4. Click the Lock/Save Sheet button at the top of the template. The Lock/Save Sheet dialog box appears, as shown in Figure 21.4. The locking options let you choose whether or not to lock the changes you made to the template. Locking the template means that you cannot edit or delete the changes you made to the template.

5. Choose a locking option, and then click OK.

Click Lock/Save Sheet to
lock and save your
customized template.

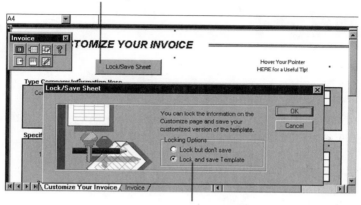

Choose a locking option.

FIGURE 21.4   Locking and saving the customized template in the Lock/Save Sheet dialog box.

6. If you chose the Lock and Don't Save option, you are returned to the customize version of the template. You cannot make changes to the template until you click on the Unlock This Sheet button at the top of the customize version of the template. In the Unlock This Sheet dialog box, click OK. Then you can make changes to the template.

7. If you chose the Lock and Save Template option, you'll see the Save As dialog box. Enter a name for the template in the File Name text box and click on Save. You are returned to the customize version of the template.

In this lesson, you learned how to create and use templates. In the next lesson, you will learn how to create charts.

LESSON 22

CREATING CHARTS

In this lesson, you will learn to create charts to represent your workbook data as a picture.

CHARTING WITH EXCEL

With Excel, you can create various types of charts. Some common chart types are shown in Figure 22.1. The chart type you choose depends on your data and on how you want to present that data. These are the major chart types and their purposes:

Pie   Use this chart to show the relationship among parts of a whole.

Bar   Use this chart to compare values at a given point in time.

Column   Similar to the Bar chart; use this chart to emphasize the difference between items.

Line   Use this chart to emphasize trends and the change of values over time.

Area   Similar to the Line chart; use this chart to emphasize the amount of change in values.

Most of these basic chart types also come in 3-dimensional varieties. In addition to looking more professional than the standard flat charts, 3-D charts can often help your audience distinguish between different sets of data.

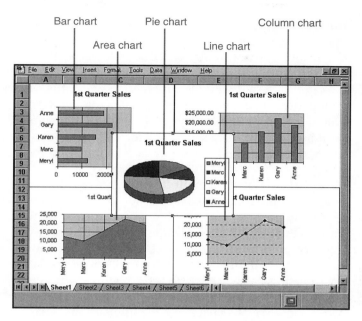

FIGURE 22.1   Commonly used Excel chart types.

 Embedded Charts   A chart that is placed on the same worksheet that contains the data used to create the chart. A chart can also be placed on a chart sheet in the workbook so that the worksheet and chart are separate. Embedded charts are useful for showing the actual data and its graphic representation side-by-side.

CHARTING TERMINOLOGY

Before you start creating charts, familiarize yourself with the following terminology:

Data Series   The bar, pie wedges, lines, or other elements that represent plotted values in a chart. For example, a chart might show a set of similar bars that reflects a series of values for the same item. The bars in the series would all have the same pattern. If you have more than one pattern of bars, each pattern would represent a separate data series. For instance, charting the sales for Territory 1 versus Territory 2 would require two data series, one for each territory. Often, data series correspond to rows of data in your worksheet.

Categories   Categories reflect the number of elements in a series. You might have two data series to compare the sales of two different territories and four categories to compare these sales over four quarters. Some charts have only one category, and others have several. Categories normally correspond to the columns that you have in your chart data, with the category labels coming from the column headings.

Axis   One side of a chart. In a two-dimensional chart, there is an X-axis (horizontal) and a Y-axis (vertical). The X-axis contains all the data series and categories in the chart. If you have more than one category, the X-axis often contains labels that define what each category represents. The Y-axis reflects the values of the bars, lines, or plot points. In a three-dimensional chart, the Z-axis represents the vertical plane, and the X-axis (distance) and Y-axis (width) represent the two sides on the floor of the chart.

Legend   Defines the separate elements of a chart. For example, the legend for a pie chart will show what each piece of the pie represents.

Gridlines   Emphasizes the Y-axis or X-axis scale of the data series. For example, major gridlines for the Y-axis will help you follow a point from the X- or Y-axis to identify a data point's exact value.

CREATING A CHART

You can create charts as part of a worksheet (an embedded chart) or as a separate chart worksheet. If you create an embedded chart, it will print side-by-side with your worksheet data. If you create a chart on a chart worksheet, you can print it separately. Both types of charts are linked to the worksheet data that they represent, so when you change the data, the chart is automatically updated.

CREATING AN EMBEDDED CHART

The ChartWizard button in the Standard toolbar allows you to create a graph frame on a worksheet. To use the ChartWizard, take the following steps:

1. Select the data you want to chart. If you typed names or other labels (for example, Qtr 1, Qtr 2, and so on) and you want them included in the chart, make sure you select them.

2. Click on the ChartWizard button in the Standard toolbar (see Figure 22.2).

3. Move the mouse pointer where you want the upper left corner of the chart to appear.

4. Hold down the mouse button, and drag to define the size and dimensions of the chart. To create a square graph, hold down the Shift key as you drag. If you want your chart to exactly fit the borders of the cells it occupies, hold down the Alt key as you drag.

5. Release the mouse button. The ChartWizard - Step 1 of 5 dialog box appears, asking if the selected range is correct. You can correct the range by typing a new range or by dragging the dialog box title bar out of the way, and dragging over the cells you want to chart.

6. Click on the Next button. The ChartWizard - Step 2 of 5 dialog box appears, as shown in Figure 22.2, asking you to select a chart type.

Chart types   ChartWizard button

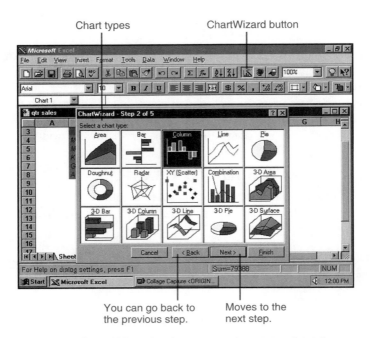

You can go back to   Moves to the
the previous step.   next step.

FIGURE 22.2   ChartWizard asks you to choose a chart type.

7. Select a chart type, and click on the Next button. The ChartWizard - Step 3 of 5 dialog box appears, asking you to select a chart format (a variation on the selected chart type).

8. Select a format for the chosen chart type, and click on the Next button. The ChartWizard - Step 4 of 5 dialog box appears, as shown in Figure 22.3. (The Column chart type and column chart format 6 were chosen to get to the dialog box in Figure 22.3. Your dialog box may look different, depending on the chart type you chose.)

9. Choose whether the data series is based on rows or columns, and choose the starting row and column. Click on the Next button. The ChartWizard - Step 5 of 5 dialog box appears.

Select whether you want data
graphed by rows or columns.

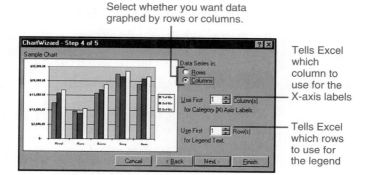

Tells Excel
which
column to
use for the
X-axis labels

Tells Excel
which rows
to use for
the legend

FIGURE 22.3   The ChartWizard prompts you to specify exactly
how you want the data charted.

10. If desired, add a legend, title, or axis labels. Click on the
    Finish button. Your completed chart appears on the cur-
    rent worksheet.

Moving and Resizing a Chart   To move an embedded
chart, click anywhere in the chart area and drag it to the
new location. To change the size of a chart, select the
chart, and then drag one of its handles (the black squares
that border the chart). Drag a corner handle to change
the height and width, or drag a side handle to change
only the width.

CREATING A CHART ON A SEPARATE WORKSHEET

If you don't want your chart to appear on the same page as your
worksheet data, you can create the chart on a separate worksheet.
To create a chart in this way, select the data you want to chart,
and then open the Insert menu, choose Chart, and choose As
New Sheet. Excel inserts a separate chart worksheet (named Chart
1) to the left of the current worksheet and starts the ChartWizard.
Perform the same steps given in the previous section for creating
a chart with the ChartWizard.

USING THE CHART TOOLBAR

You can use the Chart toolbar to create a chart, or to change an existing chart, as shown in Figure 22.4. If the Chart toolbar is not displayed, you can turn it on by choosing View Toolbars, placing a check mark in the Chart check box and clicking on OK.

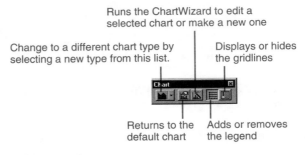

Runs the ChartWizard to edit a selected chart or make a new one

Change to a different chart type by selecting a new type from this list.

Displays or hides the gridlines

Returns to the default chart

Adds or removes the legend

FIGURE 22.4   The Chart toolbar.

SAVING CHARTS

To save a chart, simply save the workbook that contains the chart. For more details, refer to Lesson 6.

PRINTING A CHART

If a chart is an embedded chart, it will print when you print the worksheet that contains the chart. If you created a chart on a separate worksheet, you can print the chart separately by printing only the chart worksheet. For more information about printing, refer to Lesson 8.

In this lesson, you learned about the different chart types and how to create them. You also learned how to save and print charts. In the next lesson, you will learn how to turn your worksheet data into a database.

LEARNING DATABASE BASICS

In this lesson, you will learn about database basics and how to create your own database.

DATABASE BASICS

A database is a tool used for storing, organizing, and retrieving information. For example, if you want to save the names and addresses of all the people on your holiday card list, you can create a database for storing the following information for each person: first name, last name, street number, and so on. Each piece of information is entered into a separate field (cell) in the list. All of the fields for one person in the list make a record. In Excel, a cell is a field, and a row of field entries makes a record. The column headings in the list are called field names in the database. Figure 23.1 shows a database and its component parts.

Database or Data List? Excel has simplified the database operations by treating the database as a simple *list* of data. You enter the database information just like you would enter data into a worksheet. When you select a command from the Data menu, Excel recognizes the list as a database.

You must observe the following rules when you enter information into your database:

- **Field Names**: You must enter field names in the first row of the database; for example, type **First Name** for the first name, and **Last Name** for the last name. Do NOT skip a row between the field names row and the first record.

- **Records**: Each record must be in a separate row, with no empty rows between records. The cells in a given column must contain information of the same type. For example, if you have a ZIP CODE column, all cells in that column must contain a ZIP code. You can create a calculated field; one that uses information from another field of the same record and produces a result. (To do so, enter a formula, as explained in Lesson 13.)

Each row is a record.   Field names are used as column headings.

	A	B	C	D	E	F	G	H
1	Record #	First Name	Last Name	Address	City	State	ZIP Code	
2	1	Gary	Kazanjian	455 Concord Road	Boston	MA	45669	
3	2	Meryl	Heller	1345 Beverly Drive	Rocky Hill	CT	23457	
4	3	Cindy	Verga	890 Frasier Road	New York	NY	89761	
5	4	Karen	Giventer	7821 Waterston Street	Wycoff	NJ	23784	
6	5	Kim	Cohen	642 Kimball Circle	Syracuse	NY	17394	
7	6	Preston	Reese	236 West Roper	San Diego	CA	57913	
8	7	Bob	Jones	18 Country Club Road	Hampstead	NC	73315	
9	8	Melanie	Friedman	560 Lakeshore Road	Flagstaff	AZ	37426	
10	9	Terri	Digiro	7645 Snowshoe Drive	Chicago	IL	39761	
11	10	Brian	Dooney	6431 N. Buford Ave.	Minneapolis	MN	43716	
12	11	Anne	Gallo	558 Sycamore Road	Ipswich	MA	83174	
13	12	Carl	Lehmann	643 Dubrow Street	Nashua	NH	87325	
14	13	Aram	Kasparian	7423 Hampton Hill	Newport	RI	85981	
15	14	James	Lovett	6475 Central Court	Los Angeles	CA	22937	

Each cell contains a single field entry.

Figure 23.1   The parts of a database.

Record Numbering   It is a good idea to add a column that numbers the records. The record number is likely to be the only thing about the record that won't be repeated in another record, and having a unique field could come in handy in slightly more advanced databases. Also, if the records are sorted incorrectly, you can use the numbered column to restore the records to their original order.

PLANNING A DATABASE

Before you create a database, ask yourself a few questions:

- What fields make up an individual record? If you are creating the database to take the place of an existing form (a Rolodex card, information sheet, or address list), use that form to determine which fields you need.

- What is the most often referenced field in the database? (This field should be placed in the first column.)

- What is the longest entry in each column? (Use this information to set the column widths. Otherwise, you can use Format Column AutoFit Selection to have Excel adjust the column widths.)

CREATING A DATABASE

To create a database, enter data into the cells as you would enter data on any worksheet. As you enter data, follow these guidelines:

- Enter field names in the top row of the database.

- Type field entries into each cell in a single row to create a record. (You can leave a field blank, but you may run into problems later when you sort the database.)

- Do NOT leave an empty row between the field names and the records or between any records.

- If you want to enter street numbers at the beginning of the field, for example, 155 State Street, start the entry with an apostrophe so that Excel interprets the entry as text instead of as a value. However, if you want to enter, for example, One Washington Square Suite 600, you don't need the apostrophe since it begins with text.

- Keep the records on one worksheet. You cannot have a database that spans several worksheets.

Using Data Forms to Add, Edit, or Delete Records

Data forms are like index cards; there is one data form for each record in the database, as shown in Figure 23.2. You may find it easier to flip through these data form "cards" and edit entries rather than editing them as worksheet data. To display a data form, you don't select any record in your database, just open the Data menu, and select Form. You will see a data form that contains the first record in the database. The name of the database file appears at the top of the data form.

To flip from one form to the next or previous form, use the scroll bar or the ↑ and ↓ keys. To edit an entry in a record, tab to the text box that contains the entry, and type your correction. Then, press Enter. Click the Close button when you're done using the data form.

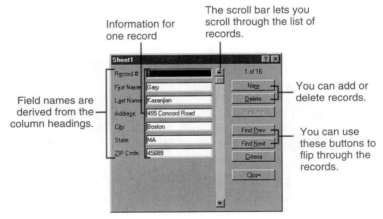

Figure 23.2   The data form.

You can also use the data form to add records to the database:

1. Open the Data menu, and choose Form to display the data form.

2. Select the New button.

3. Type an entry into each of the text boxes.

4. Click OK, or press Enter.

To delete a record:

1. Select the record you want to change by selecting the Find Prev or Find Next buttons, or by using the scroll bars or up and down arrow keys to move through the database.

2. Select Delete.

3. Click OK, or press Enter.

When you are done with the data form, click the Close button.

Template Wizard Excel for Windows 95 has a new feature called Template Wizard. This feature automatically copies the contents of cells to a database each time you save a workbook that is based on a template. To use this feature, open the Data menu, and choose Template Wizard. Follow the instructions in the Template Wizard dialog boxes to link cells in the template to your database.

In this lesson, you learned about database basics and how to create a database. In the next lesson, you will learn how to sort the database and find individual records.

24

FINDING AND SORTING DATA IN A DATABASE

In this lesson, you will learn how to sort a database and how to find individual records.

FINDING DATA WITH A DATA FORM

To find records in a database, you must specify the individual criteria (the specific information or range of information you want to find). You can look for something specific, such as red text within the form, or a condition that must be evaluated, such as all records containing sales amounts less than $1,000. Table 24.1 shows the operators that you can use for comparison:

TABLE 24.1 EXCEL'S COMPARISON OPERATORS

OPERATOR	MEANING
=	Equal to
>	Greater than
<	Less than
>=	Greater than or equal to
<=	Less than or equal to
<>	Not equal to

If you wanted to search for records containing sales amounts greater than $1,000, you would enter **>1000** in the Sales field in the criteria data form.

You can also use the following *wild cards* (characters used to represent information you don't know, or information that is common to many records) when specifying criteria:

?   Represents a single character

*   Represents multiple characters

For example, in the Name field, type **M*** to find everyone whose name begins with an M. To find everyone whose three-digit department code has 10 as the last two digits, type **?10**.

To find individual records in a database:

1. Pull down the Data menu, and select Form. The Data Form dialog box appears.

2. Click the Criteria button; the criteria data form shown in Figure 24.1 appears.

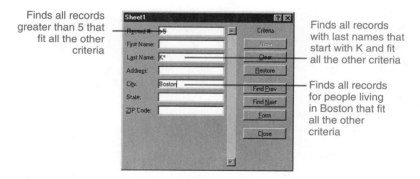

Finds all records greater than 5 that fit all the other criteria

Finds all records with last names that start with K and fit all the other criteria

Finds all records for people living in Boston that fit all the other criteria

FIGURE 24.1   Selecting search criteria.

3. Type the criteria you would like to use in the appropriate fields. Use only the fields you want to search. For example, if you want to find all Texans whose last name starts with B, type **TX** in the State field and **B*** in the Last Name field and then leave the other fields blank. The data field in which you are searching cannot be a calculated field. Excel only finds real values.

4. Select Find Next or Find Prev to look through the list of matching records.

5. When you are done reviewing records, select Close.

SORTING DATA IN A DATABASE

To sort a database, decide which field to sort by. For example, an address database could be sorted by Name or by City (or by Name within City within State). Each of these sort fields is a *key*.

You can use up to three keys when sorting your database. The first key in the above example would be State, then City, and then Name. All the names would be sorted by state. Within a state, they would be sorted by city. Within each city, the names would be sorted in alphabetical order by name. You can sort your database in ascending or descending order.

Sort Orders   Ascending order is from beginning to end, for example from A to Z or 1 to 10. Descending order is the opposite, from Z to A or 10 to 1.

To sort your database:

1. Select the area to be sorted. To sort the entire data list, select any cell in the list.

2. Pull down the Data menu, and choose Sort. The Sort dialog box appears, as shown in Figure 24.2.

3. Use the Sort By drop-down list to select the first field you want to sort on, and click on Ascending or Descending to specify a sort order.

4. To sort on another field, repeat step 3 for the first and second Then By drop-down lists.

5. Click OK, or press Enter.

You can enter up to three sorting instructions.

If you selected a header row by mistake, you can choose Header Row to omit it from the sort.

FIGURE 24.2   Selecting the sort criteria.

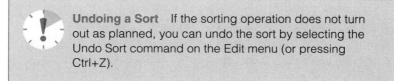

Undoing a Sort   If the sorting operation does not turn out as planned, you can undo the sort by selecting the Undo Sort command on the Edit menu (or pressing Ctrl+Z).

NARROWING YOUR LIST WITH AUTOFILTER

Excel for Windows 95 offers a feature called AutoFilter that allows you to easily display only a select group of records in your database. For example, you can display the records for only those people who live in Boston. Here's how you use AutoFilter:

1. Select the entire database, including the row you used for headings.

2. Open the Data menu, select Filter, and select AutoFilter. Excel displays drop-down list arrow buttons inside each cell at the top of your database.

3. Click on the drop-down list button for the field you want to use to filter the list. For example, if you want to display records for those people living in Boston, click on the button in the City cell. A drop-down list appears. This list contains all the entries in the column.

4. Select the entry you want to use to narrow your list. You can use the arrow keys to scroll through the list, or type the first character in the entry's name to quickly move to it. Press Enter, or click on the entry with your mouse. Excel filters the list so that only the records for the people living in Boston appear.

The Custom option in the AutoFilter drop-down list lets you apply two criteria values within the current column, or use comparison operators other than AND. To use the Custom option, click the drop-down list button for the field you want to filter, and select Custom. Excel displays the Custom AutoFilter dialog box. Enter your preferences, and choose OK to filter your data.

AutoFilter with Top 10   Excel for Windows 95's new Top 10 AutoFilter option lets you display all rows that contain the highest or lowest items in a list. (For example, the top 10% of sales revenues or the bottom 10 sales revenues.) Choose the Top 10 option in the AutoFilter drop-down list, and enter your preferences in the Top 10 AutoFilter dialog box, then choose OK to filter your data.

In this lesson, you learned how to find individual records and how to sort and filter your database. In the next lesson, you will learn how to add graphics and other objects to your worksheets.

ADDING GRAPHICS AND OTHER OBJECTS TO WORKSHEETS

25

In this lesson, you will learn how to add graphic objects to your worksheets.

WORKING WITH GRAPHIC OBJECTS

Excel comes with several tools that allow you to add graphic objects to your workbooks and charts. You can add a graphic object created in another program, you can add *clip art* (which is predrawn art that comes with Excel and other programs), or you can draw your own graphic objects using the Drawing toolbar.

 Graphic Object A graphic object is anything in your worksheet that isn't data. Graphic objects include things you can draw (such as ovals and rectangles), text boxes, charts, and clip art.

INSERTING PICTURES

If you have a collection of clip art or pictures that you created and saved using a graphics program or scanner, you can insert those pictures on a worksheet or in a chart. To insert a picture, do this:

1. Select the cell where you want to place the upper left corner of the picture. (To insert the picture in a chart, double-click on the chart to display it in a separate window.)

2. Open the Insert menu, and choose Picture. The Picture dialog box appears, as shown in Figure 25.1.

3. Change to the drive by clicking a drive in the Look In list. Then double-click on a folder in the Name list that contains your clip art or graphics files. A list of graphics files appears in the Name list.

4. Select the name of the graphics file you want to insert, and click the OK button. Excel imports the picture.

Select a file name here.

Change to the drive and folder that contains your graphic files.

This Preview button lets you see the picture in the Preview area before you insert it.

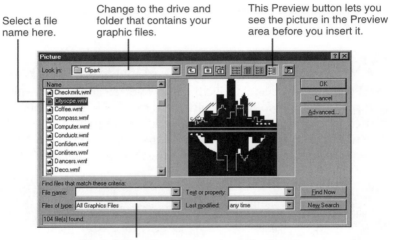

Excel displays files for several graphics formats.

FIGURE 25.1   You can insert a picture or a clip art file.

You can move the picture by dragging it. To resize the picture, drag one of its handles. Drag a corner handle to change both the width and height. Drag a side handle to change only the width, or drag a top or bottom handle to change only the height. If you decide later to move or resize your picture, simply click on the picture. The handles reappear, and you can move or resize it from there.

TIP   **Copy and Paste Pictures**   Another way to insert a picture is to copy it from one program and then paste it in Excel. First, display the picture in the program you used to create it, and use the Edit Copy command in that program to copy it to the Windows 95 Clipboard. Change back to Excel, and use the Edit Paste command to paste the picture from the Clipboard into your workbook or graph.

INSERTING OTHER OBJECTS

In addition to pictures, you can insert objects created in other programs. For example, you can insert a sound recording (if you have a sound board that has a microphone attached) or WordArt objects (if you have Microsoft Publisher or Word for Windows). When you choose to insert an object, Excel runs the required program and lets you create the object. When you quit the other program, the object is inserted on the current chart or worksheet. Here's what you do:

1. Select the cell where you want the upper left corner of the picture placed. (To insert the picture in a chart, double-click on the chart to go into edit mode.)

2. Open the Insert menu, and choose Object. The Object dialog box appears, as shown in Figure 25.2.

3. Make sure the Create New tab is up front. The Create New tab lets you run another program and create the object. The Create From File tab allows you to insert an object that you have already created and saved.

4. From the Object Type list, select the program you need to run to create the object. Remember, you must have that program installed on your computer in order for the selected program to run.

5. Click the OK button. Excel runs the selected program.

6. Use the program as you normally would to create the object. When you are done, save the object, and exit the program. When you exit, a dialog box appears asking if you want to update the link before exiting.

7. Choose Yes.

Create from File   Using the Create from File tab is sort of like using Insert Picture; both commands insert an object without running a program.

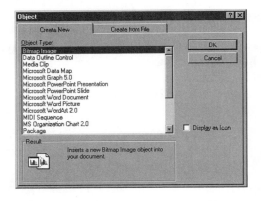

FIGURE 25.2   Select the program you need to create the object.

SHARING DATA BETWEEN APPLICATIONS WITH OLE

You can share data between applications using *Object Linking and Embedding* (OLE). Many Windows applications allow you to link and embed information in any of these applications. For example, you can copy a Microsoft Excel chart and put it into a Microsoft Word document.

OLE   OLE is an acronym for Object Linking and Embedding. This feature allows you to copy or move information between documents in different applications using drag-and-drop. Both applications must support OLE.

To share data between programs with OLE, follow these steps:

1. Open the source and destination documents in each program. Arrange the application windows so that both documents are visible.

2. Select the data you want to move or copy.

3. To move the data, drag it to the new location in the other application. To copy the data, hold down the Ctrl key and then drag the data to the new location in the other application. Release the both the mouse button and the Ctrl key.

When you copy the data, there is a link between the two copies of the data. For example, if you copy a Microsoft Excel chart into a Microsoft Word document, you can edit the chart from Microsoft Word. Just double-click on the chart in the Word document, and you are returned to Excel. You can make the changes to the chart in Excel, and Excel will automatically update the chart in the Microsoft Word document.

Drag and Drop Between Applications   Dragging and dropping data between two applications is a new feature in Windows 95 and Microsoft applications. In earlier versions of Excel, you couldn't drag and drop data between two applications.

INDEX

X–Y–Z

All the Information you need in 10 Minutes